Peterson

First Guide

to

Seashores

John Kricher

Illustrated by Gordon Morrison

HOUGHTON MIFFLIN COMPANY

Boston   New York   London

1992

For information about permission to reproduce
selections from this book, write to Permissions,
Houghton Mifflin Company, 215 Park Avenue
South, New York, New York 10003.

Library of Congress Cataloging-in-Publication Data

Kricher, John C.
    Peterson first guide to seashores / John
Kricher ; illustrated by Gordon Morrison
        p.   cm. — (Peterson first guide series)
    Includes index.
    ISBN 0-395-61901-7
    1. Seashore fauna— Identification. 2. Sea-
shore flora— Identification. I. Title. II. Series.
QH95.7.K75   1992
574.909'46--dc20   91-38829
                                            CIP

Printed in Italy

NWI 10 9 8 7 6 5 4 3 2 1

Editor's Note

In 1934, my *Field Guide to the Birds* first saw the light of day. This book was designed so that live birds could be readily identified at a distance, by their patterns, shapes, and field marks, without resorting to the technical points specialists use to name species in the hand or in the specimen tray. The book introduced the "Peterson System," as it is now called, a visual system based on patternistic drawings with arrows to pinpoint the key field marks. The system is now used throughout the Peterson Field Guide series, which has grown to over 40 volumes on a wide range of subjects, from ferns to fishes, rocks to stars, animal tracks to edible plants.

Even though Peterson Field Guides are intended for the novice as well as the expert, there are still many beginners who would like something simpler to start with— a smaller guide that would give them confidence. It is for this audience— those who perhaps recognize a crow or a robin, buttercup or daisy, but little else— that the Peterson First Guides have been created. They offer a selection of the animals and plants you are most likely to see during your first forays afield. By narrowing the choices— and using the Peterson System— they make identification much easier. First Guides make it easy to get started in the field, and easy to graduate to the full-fledged Peterson Field Guides.

Roger Tory Peterson

About This Book

We travel to the shore not only to swim in the surf, but to beachcomb and to get a glimpse of life in the vast deep oceans that cover 71% of earth's surface. What kind of crab is that? What are those birds diving in the waves? Is that a seaweed? What kind of fish did that angler just haul in? When you learn to identify some of the plants and animals, you begin to ask how they interact. Soon you begin to realize that the whole is more than the sum of its parts. You become an environmentalist.

First Guide to Seashores is an introduction to the diverse and wonderful forms of life that live along our shores. With keen eyes, perhaps binoculars and a small magnifying glass, and, of course, no aversion to getting your feet wet, you can take this book into the field and introduce yourself to many of the most fascinating forms of life on the planet.

Our coastal environments are among our most precious resources. They are also among our most fragile environments. Threatened by pollution and overbuilding, seashores are often not appreciated until it is too late. It is our hope that this little book will help you better understand and appreciate our seashores and that you will contribute to their preservation and protection.

Where land meets ocean

The seashore is often a rigorous environment, subject to salt spray, winds, pounding waves, and shifting sands. At the same time, however, it presents many opportunities for organisms. Rivers carry sediments rich in nutrients, depositing them in bays, estuaries, and salt marshes. Many kinds of plants and animals anchor themselves on rocks, piers, and pilings. As you wander along seashores, take note of the many ways plants and animals survive in this narrow space between land and sea. Inspect shells and driftwood washed up from the sea, for there may be many odd creatures attached. Beachcombing is fun no matter what the season. Summer is fine for sun worshipers, but winter storms wash many oddities of the sea ashore. Put on warm clothes and brave the winds.

Intertidal Zone. Seashore dwellers must adapt to the changes caused by the rhythmic motion of the tides. Many organisms live between the points of high tide and low tide, an area called the intertidal zone. When the tide is in (high tide) these organisms feed on the bounty brought by the rich coastal waters. When the tide goes out, waste products are washed out to sea, and eggs and larvae are dispersed by the sea. However, when the tide is out (low tide), these creatures, which must stay moist, are forced to "shut down." Beach-combing is quite rewarding during low tide. You can poke among the seaweeds, rock crevices, and tide pools, and see all manner of animals waiting it out until the next high tide. Because plants and animals differ in their abilities to tolerate exposure to air, the inter-tidal zone is usually divided into a series of zones. As you pass from low water line to high water line you'll find a zone of brown algae, a zone of blue mussels, a barnacle zone, and perhaps a zone of green algae. If you can use a mask and snorkel, high tide is ideal for looking at the intertidal zone.

Kinds of Plants

Land plants. Many land plants are adapted to withstand salt spray and evaporation caused by winds from off the ocean. Botanizing on sand dunes or in a salt marsh is an ideal way to get acquainted with these species.

Algae. Everyone who goes to the seashore has seen "seaweeds." These plants must remain moist or they will perish. All algae lack the stiff tissues of land plants and need water to hold them up. Most feel slick, if not slimy, to the touch. Some can be eaten and are quite tasty and filled with vitamins.

Phytoplankton. These marine plants are too small to be seen without a microscope. Often called the grasses of the sea, they sustain the food chains of the open ocean.

Kinds of Animals

All the major animal groups evolved in the sea, and most are still there. Members of only a few groups, particularly the joint-legged animals and those with backbones, have adapted to land. The many different kinds of marine creatures fall into several major groups.

Coelenterates. These are the jellyfish, sea anemones, corals, and hydroids, such as the Portuguese Man-Of-War. Many invade shallow bays or wash up on beaches, where, because they lack shells or skeletons, they resemble limp globs of mucus. Anemones attach to rocks and pilings. Corals form vast reefs in tropical waters. All coelenterates have a simple body structure, with but a single opening through which food enters and waste products are eliminated. Tentacles are armed with stinging cells that capture food.

Segmented Worms. In the world of mud and sand, worms and clams are the most abundant animals. Many kinds of segmented worms, or annelids, burrow in marine sediments. Related to the terrestrial earthworm, marine worms range from active, graceful swimmers to odd-looking tube dwellers that sweep the mud with moplike tentacles.

Mollusks. These are the snails, clams, mussels, squids, octopuses, and chitons. Mollusks have a muscular foot, and most make shells of calcium carbonate. Some are among our tastiest delicacies of the sea. Some snails are predators, feeding on clams, barnacles, and mussels. Others are herbivores, feeding like little marine cows on tiny algae that grow on rocks. Clams and mussels stay put, filtering the water to extract oxygen and food. Squid and octopuses, with eyes strikingly like our own, are active, swimming by their own version of jet propulsion in quest of fish and other food morsels. Scientists have learned that octopuses and squids are among the most intelligent invertebrate animals.

Arthropods. The name of this highly successful group means "joint-legged." Arthropods also have an external skeleton, which must be shed at intervals so that they can grow. The most diverse arthropods are the insects, almost all of which live on land. In the sea, the *crustaceans* are the biggest group of arthropods. They include shrimps, lobsters, crabs, and barnacles. Most have tiny larvae that are part of the hordes of *zooplankton* (tiny, floating animals) and some, like the copepods (page 76), are members of the zooplankton even as adults.

Echinoderms. Echinoderms are spiny-skinned ocean dwellers that are usually rounded, with their bodies separated into five parts. They include the sea stars (starfish), sea urchins, and sea cucumbers. Some of them are voracious predators, devouring clams and other shellfish. Others feed on the decaying matter on the surface of mud.

Tunicates. These are baglike creatures that may, at first, be mistaken for sea anemones. Their larvae are like tadpoles and are thus very similar to tiny fish, with gills, a stiff backbone and a nerve cord like our own. The first fish, which appeared about 500 million years ago, may have evolved from tunicate larvae.

Vertebrates. These are animals with backbones. They include the bony fish, sharks and rays, sea turtles, marine mammals, and seabirds. Their large size makes them among the most noticeable marine animals. We'll meet many of them in this book.

Northeastern Rocky Coast

The northeastern rocky coastline extends from Canada to southern New England. Waves from the cold sea crash over huge granite boulders, where numerous plants and animals attach tightly to avoid washing away. Protected tide pools also harbor many kinds of marine life that serve as food for coastal-dwelling birds.

The Intertidal Zone

A look at the granite boulders reveals different zones between the tidelines, a result of the various degrees to which marine plants and animals can tolerate exposure during low tide. The lower the zone, the more it remains under water, but the higher zones are exposed to drying sun and winds much of the time, so only the hardiest creatures can survive.

The highest intertidal zone is the *barnacle zone*. Each barnacle is permanently housed in a *small crater* of its own making, and it can never move from its point of attachment.When the tide is out, the barnacle tightly closes its shell, a protection against drying.

ACORN BARNACLES   **To 1 in.**

The many species of acorn barnacles encrust rocks, boat bottoms, and even whales. These little crustaceans feed by waving their *jointed, netlike legs* in the water, entrapping tiny marine organisms.

Beneath the barnacle zone is the *brown algae zone*, where thick clumps of slick algae attach. These *golden-brown* plants have small air bladders that help them to float and absorb wave pounding.

ROCKWEED   **To 3 ft.**

This brown alga has broad, flat blades, with a clear midrib stripe. Its pea-shaped air bladders pop when you step on them.

KNOTTED WRACK   **To 2 ft.**

An *olive* alga with narrow blades and short branches. The "knots" are air bladders.

ACORN BARNACLES

ROCKWEED

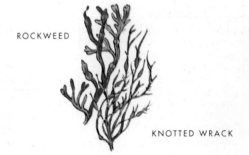

KNOTTED WRACK

The two lowest intertidal zones are the *Irish Moss zone* and the *Kelp zone*. These zones are exposed to air only when the tide is very low. Kelp includes several species of large algae, all of which are rich brown in color.

Algae grow very quickly, because they receive lots of sunlight in addition to rich nutrients from sea water. The colors of red and brown algae help them survive. Brown and red pigments receive sunlight under water much better than the green pigment chlorophyll. The energy from the sunlight is then "passed on" to chlorophyll so that the plant can photosynthesize successfully.

The dense jungle of brown and red algae provides vital habitat for many kinds of animals that live within the various zones.

IRISH MOSS   To 7 in.
A red alga found on rocks at low-tide mark. Usually *deep purple-red*. Blades flattened with *multiple small branches*. Like other seaweeds, Irish Moss is rich in vitamins, and can be cooked into a jelly or made into soup.

DULSE   To 12 in.
A red alga with a wide, flattened blade with *little branching*. Dulse can be made into a tasty pudding or dried into a snack food.

HORSETAIL KELP   To 3½ ft.
Each wide, ribless frond of this brown seaweed is split into many "fingers."

SEA COLANDER   To 6 ft.
Long fronds with a prominent midrib. The blades are rather like Swiss cheese, with *numerous holes*.

EDIBLE KELP   To 10 ft.
A tasty seaweed with long, wavy-edged fronds. The thinly sliced midribs can be added to salad, and the *narrow blades* at the base can be dried and used as seasoning or to make soup.

IRISH MOSS

DULSE

SEA COLANDER

HORSETAIL KELP

EDIBLE KELP

Birds of the East Coast

HERRING GULL   23–26 in.

This robust gull is abundant along eastern coastal areas. Adult birds are white with *gray wings and back.* The wings have *black tips.* The yellow bill has a red spot on the end of the lower part. It takes four years for Herring Gulls to develop their adult plumage; they are brown in their first year. Known for their loud ringing calls.

GREATER BLACK-BACKED   28–31 in.
GULL

Larger than the Herring Gull, with a *black* upper back, or "mantle." These gulls feed on almost anything, from baby birds such as terns to dead fish. They are present summer and winter, and have expanded their populations in recent years, feeding on garbage from the ever-increasing human population.

DOUBLE-CRESTED CORMORANT   33 in.

A black, goose-sized bird with a sharply hooked *orange-yellow bill,* often seen with its *wings spread* as it dries them in the sun after diving for fish. Other birds' feathers are covered with a natural oil that repels water. Cormorants, however, have little oil on their feathers and need to dry them.

ATLANTIC PUFFIN   12 in.

The chunky black and white puffin, also called the "sea parrot," can carry several fish at once in its wide *red, blue, and yellow bill.* Atlantic Puffins live in large colonies on offshore islands and along cliffs, where they nest in burrows among the rocks. Puffins have been reintroduced on Maine islands and may one day become more common.

BLACK GUILLEMOT   12–14 in.

Black with *white wing patches* and a narrow, *pointed* bill. Like puffins, guillemots dive for fish. Puffins and guillemots somewhat resemble penguins.

GREATER BLACK-
BACKED GULL

HERRING GULL

DOUBLE-CRESTED
CORMORANT

ATLANTIC
PUFFIN

BLACK
GUILLEMOT

Rocky-coast Snails

COMMON PERIWINKLE   1¹/₂ in.
The most abundant and largest periwinkle.
Brown with a *pale lip* and *blunt spire*. This
snail has spread to North America from
Europe. It can remain out of water for long
periods, tucked safely in its shell.

ROUGH PERIWINKLE   ¹/₂ in.
Similar but smaller than the Common Periwinkle, with *tiny grooves* in its grayish
brown shell. The female snail keeps her eggs
safely within her body, and "gives birth" to
live young when the eggs hatch.

SMOOTH PERIWINKLE   ¹/₂ in.
The most colorful of the three periwinkle
species, often *bright orange or yellow*. Also
has the most *rounded shell* of any periwinkle. These periwinkles are often hidden
among the dense fronds of Rockweed and
other algae.

TORTOISESHELL LIMPET   1 in.
Limpets are rounded, *flat* snails. Their
shape allows them to adhere tightly to the
rockface and tolerate wave pounding
without washing away. The animal's name
refers to its *ornate brown and white pattern*
and its shape. Limpets eat algae.

DOGWINKLE   1¹/₂ in.
This common snail is highly variable in
color. Most are white, but you'll find some to
be yellow, orange, brown, or white with
brown banding. Dogwinkles are the "wolves"
of the intertidal zone, devouring both barnacles and mussels by drilling into them with
a raspy tongue.

RED-GILLED NUDIBRANCH   1¹/₂ in.
Nudibranchs are snails that lack shells.
The name means "naked gills," a reference
to the many clublike protrusions called
cerata that are used for respiration. This
species has *reddish cerata*.

COMMON
PERIWINKLE

ROUGH
PERIWINKLE

SMOOTH
PERIWINKLE

TORTOISESHELL
LIMPET

DOGWINKLE

RED-GILLED
NUDIBRANCH

Rocky-shore Echinoderms

FORBES' ASTERIAS   5–8 in.
This is one of several common sea stars, or
starfish, that occur along the East Coast
and the Gulf of Mexico. It is *reddish* with an
orange spot. This spot, the madreporite,
controls water in and out of the animal,
providing suction for its tube feet. Sea stars
prey on clams and mussels, which they
open by steadily pulling the shell apart with
their hundreds of tiny suction-tube feet. The
sea star then slides its stomach into the
opened mollusk and digests it!

BLOOD STAR   2–4 in.
There are several species of blood stars,
each very similar to the others. As the name
implies, these sea stars are usually *bright
red,* though some may be orange or yellow.
Look for them in tide pools, where they feed
on sponges.

GREEN SEA URCHIN   3 in.
This *olive-green* sea urchin resembles a
prickly ball, though its spines are quite
blunt and it is easy to pick up. It feeds on
algae, which it scrapes off rocks. Its tube
feet help it hang on to the rockface through
heavy waves. Sea uchin shells, called tests,
lose their spines when the animal dies.

ORANGE-FOOTED SEA   10 in.
CUCUMBER
Although this odd animal can grow to
almost a foot in length, individuals found in
tide pools are usually smaller. It captures
tiny animals with its bushy tentacles. It is
the only sea cucumber with *orange feet.*

BASKET STAR   10 in.
This unmistakable creature is mostly a
deep-water animal, though some wash into
the intertidal zone. Each of the five arms is
divided into *many branches* and may be up
to 18 inches long. The color may be yellow,
cream, or rich brown.

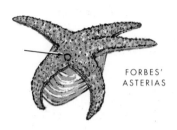

FORBES'
ASTERIAS

BLOOD
STAR

GREEN
SEA URCHIN

ORANGE-FOOTED
SEA CUCUMBER.

BASKET STAR

Rocky-shore Crustaceans

ROCK CRAB 5 in.

With its *orange-brown* shell almost half a
foot across, this is the largest of the rocky-
shore crabs. Its claws are strong so be
careful— this crab can give quite a pinch.
Look for them in rock crevices or in tide
pools. They feed on dead fish and small
invertebrates.

GREEN CRAB 3 in.

This common species has a *light green shell*
with *dark botches*. It is pale orange under-
neath. Look closely at the underside of a
crab. The crab's abdomen is folded tightly
against its underside, the tip near the crab's
mouth, and looks like part of the lower shell.
Green Crabs frequent many kinds of habi-
tats and can live in almost fresh water. Like
other crabs, they are scavengers.

NORTHERN LOBSTER To 3 ft.

Most famous as a table delicacy, the
Northern Lobster is normally greenish with
orange patches, though it turns bright red
when boiled. The *two large claws differ:* one
has blunt points along its inner edge, used
for crushing shells, the other has sharp
points for pinching and holding prey.
Lobsters are found mostly offshore, where
they live among rocks and in crevices. They
are caught in baited lobster traps. Those
that avoid the trap keep growing, and some
giants can weigh over 40 pounds. Occasionally, bright blue lobsters are found.

BOREAL RED SHRIMP 5 in.

This shrimp is partial to deeper waters.
Schools of them are hunted from boats
called trawlers, which catch shrimp by the
thousands in large nets. Red shrimp are
often served as "prawns." The *red* color
helps protect the shrimp in deep water: Red
wavelengths of light fail to penetrate into
deep water, thus a red animal does not
reflect light, making it nearly invisible.

ROCK CRAB

GREEN CRAB

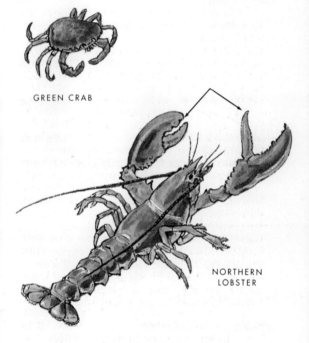

NORTHERN
LOBSTER

BOREAL
RED SHRIMP

Offshore Birds and Mammals

COMMON LOON   **28–36 in.**

A goose-sized bird with a *long, straight bill.*
The bird is gray in winter, the time at which
it is found along the coastline. In summer,
Common Loons have a blackish green head
and a black and white checkered back. They
nest on inland lakes.

HORNED GREBE   **12–15 in.**

Also a winter visitor to the coast, this bird is
the size of a small duck. It has a *pointed bill,
white cheeks,* and *black cap.* If you get to see
it closely, look for the bright red eyes.
Horned Grebes nest in the arctic. In their
summer plumage, they have bright yellow
feather tufts on their cheeks.

COMMON EIDER   **23–27 in.**

A large oceanic duck that dives for mussels
and clams. Males are boldly patterned in
black and white with a *greenish yellow bill.*
Females are grayish brown. Many hundreds
of eiders may flock together on the ocean, in
groups known as rafts.

HARBOR SEAL   **5 ft.**

Head *doglike,* without obvious ears. Seals
are commonly spotted reclining atop an
exposed rock, or submerged, with only their
head or even just a nose out of water.
Harbor seals, which can weigh up to 250
pounds, are fast swimmers and feed on fish.

FINBACK WHALE   **To 70 ft.**

From a rocky New England shore, it is often
possible to see whale spouts offshore. One
of the larger whales, the Finback is named
for its *small dorsal fin.* It feeds by filtering
small fish and other tiny animals out of the
water with the horny "baleen" in its mouth.
The whale's spout is caused by its exhaled
breath: whales are mammals and must
surface to breathe air just as we do.

COMMON LOON

summer

winter

COMMON EIDER

HORNED GREBE

HARBOR SEAL

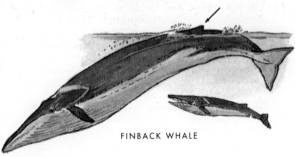

FINBACK WHALE

A Dock Piling

Low tide reveals the many kinds of marine organisms that make their homes here.

SEA LETTUCE To 3 ft.

A *bright green, sheetlike* algae that often attaches to rocks exposed to waves. It can be chopped and added to salads.

FRILLED ANEMONE , 4 in.

A common sea anemone with *white tentacles* found in New England. Though they resemble plants when open, anemones are coelenterates, related to jellyfish. The flowerlike tentacles contain hundreds of stinging cells.

NORTHERN RED ANEMONE 2–3 in.

This anemone has *red tentacles* and a brownish stalk usually steaked with green. When exposed, anemones contract their tentacles and resemble blobs of jelly.

SEA GRAPES $^1/_2$ in.

These animals, looking like a *cluster of grapes* often covered with debris, are sea squirts, a kind of tunicate. These baglike animals siphon water through their bodies, filtering out plankton. The larval sea squirt looks like a tiny tadpole, and is very similar to a fish.

SEA VASE $2^1/_2$ in.

This sea squirt is often solitary, mostly *transparent* and yellowish.

BLUE MUSSEL 4 in.

Often grows in huge numbers, covering rocks and pilings. Named for its *slate blue* shells. Mussels make very strong threads with which they anchor themselves to anything solid. Also called the Edible Mussel; good to eat when the water is not polluted.

RED BEARD SPONGE To 8 in.

Often encrusts pilings. Its many *bright red branches* filter water, extracting plankton.

SEA LETTUCE

BARNACLES

FRILLED ANEMONE

NORTHERN RED ANEMONE

SEA GRAPES

SEA VASE

RED BEARD SPONGE

BLUE MUSSELS

Rocky-coast Fishes

ATLANTIC COD   **To 6 ft.**
Cod is one of the staple seafoods of New
England. These fish can weigh up to 200
pounds. Cod have *three upper fins,* a well-
marked *line along their sides,* and a *single
barbel,* or "whisker," on the chin. They are
caught in large schools offshore, on such
fishing grounds as Georges Bank and the
Grand Banks. Cod vary in color: most are
greenish yellow, but some are reddish. All
cod have *many spots* on their body.

SAND LANCE   **4–6 in.**
Small *pencil-shaped* fish with a *long upper
fin.* Lower jaw larger than upper jaw. Found
in large schools just offshore. Serves as food
for seabirds, whales, and porpoises.

TAUTOG   **3 ft.**
A stout fish, grayish brown and greenish,
with dark blotches and a *long, spiny upper
fin.* It feeds on mussels and crabs, which it
crushes with its strong jaws and teeth.
Tautog inhabit rocky shores, breakwaters,
ledges, and shipwrecks.

GOLDEN REDFISH   **2 ft.**
This colorful fish inhabits rocky bottoms
from shallow to deep water. They are *orange*
to *bright red,* with *large black eyes.* They
have sharp spines on the fin that runs along
their upper back. They eat mostly shrimp,
other crustaceans, and small fish.

GOOSEFISH   **4 ft.**
A fish that somewhat resembles a frog. It
has a *huge, flattened head* and *wide mouth*
studded with sharp teeth. Goosefish can
weigh up to 50 pounds. You can often find
them in shallow water along the tideline, but
they also inhabit deep water. They use their
long head spine as a fishing pole, complete
with bait, to lure small fish. Often sold
under the name "monkfish."

ATLANTIC COD

SAND LANCE

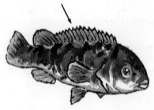

TAUTOG

GOLDEN
REDFISH

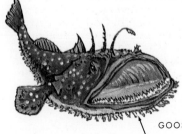

GOOSEFISH

Jellyfish

Jellyfish are coelenterates, relatives of sea anemones and corals. They drift about on the surface of the ocean, using their weak muscles to move against the currents. Many are caught in the waves and stranded on beaches. Jellyfish capture fish and other prey with the stinging cells on their tentacles, which hang beneath the transparent bell.

MOON JELLY   To 10 in.

Often seen in immense numbers along the eastern coast. Mostly transparent, but has *four horseshoe-shaped rings* in its center that are actually its reproductive organs. In males these are pink, and in females they are white. Tentacles *short*.

PURPLE JELLYFISH   2 in.

A deep-water species that sometimes invades bays and washes ashore. It is small, with *eight long purplish tentacles* and a *maroon red bell*.

SEA NETTLE   4–7 in.

Like the plant of the same name, Sea Nettle can give an irritating, painful sting. It is often found in bays and estuaries, and swimmers should avoid it. Mostly transparent, Sea Nettle has *pale orange tentacles*. Found from Cape Cod south.

LION'S MANE   To 8 ft.

The largest jellyfish in our area, though most are considerably smaller than the 8-foot maximum. Also known as Red Jelly, its northern populations are *bright red,* while those to the south tend to be *paler orange and yellow.*

MOON JELLY

PURPLE
JELLYFISH

SEA
NETTLE

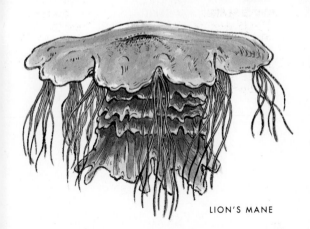

LION'S MANE

Hydroids

What looks like a single animal is actually a complex colony of individuals, each with a certain task. Other animals may also live in the colonies.

TUBULARIAN HYDROIDS   6 in.
These common intertidal hyroids look like plants. The main feeding bodies, called polyps, have several *flowerlike rings of tentacles.*

STRIPED NUDIBRANCH   1 in.
Nudibranchs are small snails without shells. They often feed on the polyps of tubularians. This species is *rusty brown.*

SKELETON SHRIMP $^1/_2$ in.
Not a true shrimp, this small, *skinny* animal climbs about among the hyroids, seeking out tiny prey.

ANGLED HYDROMEDUSA   Less than 1 in.
This hydroid looks like a tiny jellyfish. Less than an inch wide, it has up to *80 tentacles,* each of which is an individual organism. Mostly translucent, this hydromedusa is strongly tinged with *yellow.*

PORTUGUESE MAN-OF-WAR   12 in.
An infamous hydroid because of its potentially deadly sting. This warm-water hydroid has a *balloon-like float* 12 inches long and *stinging tentacles* that can extend 50 feet. The stinging cells on the tentacles are among the most powerful of any hydroid. Though dangerous, it is beautiful, with shades of lavender and pink on the float and tentacles, and bright *pinkish red* along the *upper margin* of the float. Portuguese Man-of-War often wash ashore, but beware: even a beached one can sting.

BY-THE-WIND SAILOR   4 in.
A small *bluish* hydroid often found in the warm Gulf Stream. The float has a *sail,* and the stinging tentacles are short.

TUBULARIAN HYDROIDS

STRIPED NUDIBRANCH

SKELETON SHRIMP

ANGLED HYDROMEDUSA

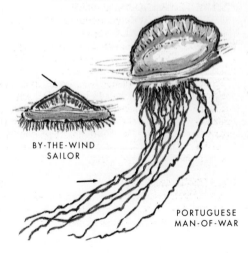

BY-THE-WIND SAILOR

PORTUGUESE MAN-OF-WAR

Eastern Sandy Beaches

A day at the beach is one of the finest forms of relaxation: warm sand, salt spray, and black-hooded **Laughing Gulls** overhead, giving their loud, nearly hysterical calls. The **Common Tern,** a small, slender bird with pointed wings and a forked tail, may often be seen picking fish from the water. It is related to the smaller **Least Tern**. Terns nest in colonies in dunes.

Flocks of **Sanderlings** scurry at the waves' edge, picking up tiny animals exposed by waves. In spring they are reddish, but they turn gray as they return from their Arctic nesting grounds in midsummer. Many walkers fail to notice the little **Piping Plover** until it gives its "piping" call. Pale gray above and white below, the plover seems to melt into the sand when sitting on its nest near the dunes.

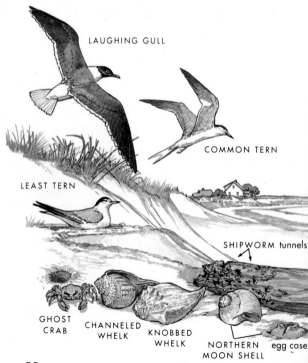

LAUGHING GULL

COMMON TERN

LEAST TERN

SHIPWORM tunnels

GHOST CRAB

CHANNELED WHELK

KNOBBED WHELK

NORTHERN MOON SHELL

egg case

BEACH FLEAS

MOLE CRAB

COQUINA CLAMS

TRUMPET WORM

Beyond the Waves

LADY CRAB   3 in.

This crab is common in waters with sandy bottoms, and its shed shell, or carapace, is often washed ashore. It is a swimming crab, and its last pair of legs has segments that are *flattened* into paddles. The shell is mottled purplish or reddish brown, and the *claws are orange.* Like most crabs, Ladys scavenge for food.

BLUE CRAB   9 in.

The Blue Crab, a popular delicacy of the Chesapeake Bay region, is one of the most important contributors to the eastern shellfish industry. Like the Lady Crab, it is a swimming crab. Its powerful claws can give a sharp pinch. The shell is olive, but the *legs and claws* are *bright blue* fringed with orange. Blue Crabs live offshore and in estuaries.

MANTIS SHRIMP   10 in.

This formidable-looking animal is not often seen, for it burrows in sand below the tide-line and is active mostly at night. Named for its vague resemblance to a praying mantis, Mantis Shrimp, like their insect namesakes, are voracious predators of shrimp, fish, and anything else they can catch in their formidable front appendages. Mantis Shrimp have *brilliant green eyes.*

SEA MOUSE   9 in.

This unusual-looking creature is not a mouse but a wide-bodied worm covered with a *colorful furry coat* and tiny bristles. The "fur" glistens with iridescent greens, browns, and golds. It lives offshore, combing the bottom for food, but is sometimes washed ashore after a severe storm. The Sea Mouse's scientific name, *Aphrodita*, comes from the Greek goddess Aphrodite— an odd name for a fat worm.

LADY
CRAB

BLUE
CRAB

MANTIS
SHRIMP

SEA
MOUSE

Delaware Bay

ATLANTIC HORSESHOE CRAB   To 24 in.

This prehistoric animal has scarcely changed since it appeared over 300 million years ago, even before the dinosaurs evolved. It has a wide shell and a *long spike-like tail*. It uses its *five pairs of legs* to move and to pick up prey, tiny clams and worms. Its gills, arranged like pages of a book, show that its most close relatives are spiders and scorpions. In late spring, during the highest tides, thousands of Atlantic Horseshoe Crabs gather along the beaches of Delaware Bay to mate and lay eggs. The billions of pale green eggs serve as a key food for several species of migrant shorebirds, providing them essential fuel for their flight north to their Arctic breeding grounds.

SLIPPER SHELL   1 in.

Slipper Shells are frequently seen attached to the shells of Atlantic Horseshoe Crabs. Slipper Shells are snails whose shells are *smooth and flattened* to stick tightly on a surface. Often several Slippers are attached, one atop another. The lower ones are females, the upper ones males.

RED KNOT   10–11 in.

This sandpiper is chunky and robust, with a *short black bill* and *greenish legs.* Red Knots by the thousands are attracted to Horseshoe Crab eggs that wash up along Delaware Bay's eastern shore each spring. The Red Knot is bright *reddish orange* in spring when migrating north to its Arctic breeding grounds. Its plumage is gray when it flies south in late summer.

RUDDY TURNSTONE   8–10 in.

The Ruddy Turnstone is *orange-red* with a *harlequin pattern* of black and white on its face and bright *orange legs.* The name "turnstone" comes from the bird's habit of probing in gravel and sand for food.

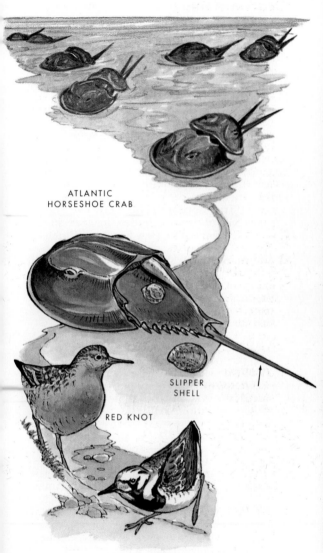

ATLANTIC
HORSESHOE CRAB

SLIPPER
SHELL

RED KNOT

RUDDY
TURNSTONE

Swift Swimmers of the Open Sea

STRIPED BASS   To 5 ft.

Silver with *7–8 black stripes* running the length of the body. The Striped Bass is one of the most popular game fishes, often caught by surfcasting with a rod and reel. A fully grown adult can weigh up to 50 pounds. Striped Bass, also known as Rockfish, spawn in estuaries and rivers. Some populations have been reduced by pollution.

BLUEFISH   3 ft.

A sleek *silvery blue* fish with a *large mouth.* The first dorsal fin is small and spiny. Bluefish are among the most popular table treats. They appear in Florida by mid-winter and move northward, satisfying seafood lovers all the way to New England. Bluefish are the "wolf packs" of the ocean: they attack schools of smaller fish with their powerful jaws and sharp teeth. Occasionally, swimmers at northeastern beaches are bitten by Bluefish who mistake the swimmers for food. Adults can weigh up to 25 pounds.

ATLANTIC BONITO   To 3 ft.

This streamlined member of the tuna family is steel bluish above and silvery yellow below, with *7 or more stripes* along each side. It is also a popular table fish, often caught with a rod and reel.

LONG-FINNED SQUID   25 in.

Squid are compact, shaped a bit like bullets, with *10 tentacles, large eyes,* and *winglike fins* along their sides. This species is often preyed upon by Bluefish and tuna. Squid are mollusks, closely related to octopuses, but much more streamlined and swift. They can swim equally well fowards or backwards. They have excellent eyesight, and have eyes very much like our own. They capture food with their 10 tentacles armed with suction cups.

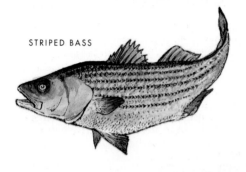

STRIPED BASS

LONG-FINNED
SQUID

BLUEFISH

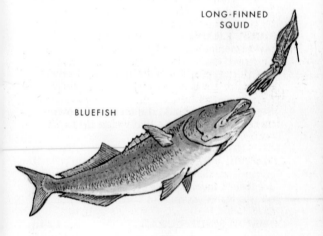

ATLANTIC
BONITO

Mudflats, Oyster Bars, and Eelgrass Flats

Around salt marshes, bays, and estuaries, vast expanses of mudflats are revealed at low tide. Armed with shovel and pail and a willingness to get muddy feet, the beachcomber can find an abundance of burrowing creatures.

GREEN FLEECE   To 3 ft.

A green alga or seaweed introduced from Europe to the mid-Atlantic seashore. It grows in estuaries and is commonly washed up on flats. This *bright green* plant has many *spongy* branches. It sometimes grows so dense that it can choke shellfish beds.

HERMIT CRABS   1 in.

Most species are *pinkish* with *orange legs*. The crab carefully chooses an empty snail shell, then tucks its soft abdomen into the shell and carries it about as it ambles the flats in search of food. If danger threatens, the crab pulls inside the shell and blocks the entrance with its *thick front claws.*

MUD SHRIMP   To 4 in.

Several species of mud shrimp build communal burrows in mud. These *pale gray* creatures rarely leave their burrows, feeding on plankton washed in with the tides.

COMMON SPIDER CRAB   12 in.

Spider crabs are often seen crawling about over mudflats. They look menacing but are quite harmless: their claws can barely pinch. These crabs have a 4-inch *spiny shell*, often yellowish in color. They can also be identified by their *long legs.* They feed on whatever organic matter they can find.

NORTHERN STARGAZER   To 20 in.

This odd fish is always looking up, with its *eyes located on the top of its head.* It buries itself in muddy sand. Be careful: just behind its eyes are special muscles capable of giving an electric shock.

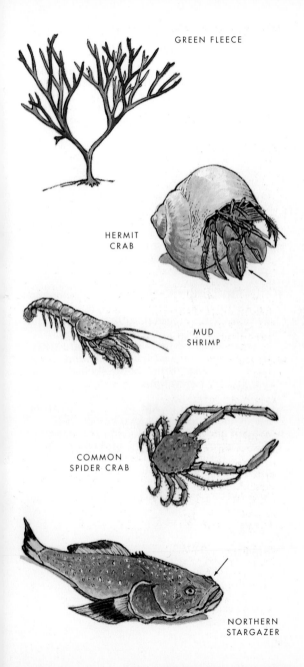

GREEN FLEECE

HERMIT
CRAB

MUD
SHRIMP

COMMON
SPIDER CRAB

NORTHERN
STARGAZER

Shellfish of the Flats

Some of our tastiest seafood morsels come from mudflats. Other species, less tempting to the palate, share the mud. All clams are filter-feeders—water goes in through one siphon tube, food and oxygen are filtered out, and the water goes out through another siphon tube. Look for clam burrows across mudflats at low tide.

SOFT-SHELLED CLAM 4 in.

Also known as "steamer" and "gaper," this clam burrows deeply, extending its long, grayish pink siphons to the surface of its burrow. As you walk across a mudflat, you might get squirted as the clams detect your vibrations in the mud. Like most burrowing clams, soft-shells use their pinkish, wedge-shaped muscular foot to dig. As the name implies, the *white shell* breaks easily.

HARD-SHELLED CLAM 4 in.

Another palate pleaser, the "quahog" is usually found in less muddy areas than the Soft-shelled Clam, and makes shallow burrows because its *siphon tubes are short.* Its shells are thick with a *purple band* on the inside rear edge. Small Hard-shelled Clams are called "cherrystones."

COMMON RAZOR CLAM 10 in.

Easily identified by its *long bluish shell,* shaped like an old-fashioned razor case. They burrow quite deeply, and by rapidly disappearing into their burrows can easily escape the would-be clammer.

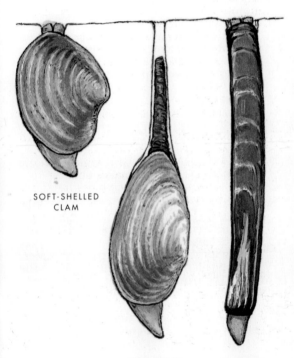

SOFT-SHELLED
CLAM

HARD-SHELLED
CLAM

COMMON
RAZOR CLAM

STOUT TAGELUS   4 in.

Also called the Stout Razor Clam, this is an
abbreviated version of the Common Razor
Clam. Its siphons are *long* and more separated than in other species. The shell is
white but partly covered by brown material
called the periostracum, which helps protect
the shell. The Tagelus is found in muddy
areas throughout the intertidal zone as well
as in shallow waters. It makes permanent
mucus-lined burrows.

BALTIC MACOMA   1 1/2 in.

This small clam has an *oval-shaped, pinkish
white* shell and long siphons that sweep the
surface of the mud like a vacuum cleaner
picking up microscopic food.

GEM SHELL   Less than 1/2 in.

Thousands of these *tiny, purplish white*
clams live together in just a few square
yards, all buried in shallow mud. They do
not burrow deeply, but they can disappear
into the mud with amazing speed. They too
feed on microscopic creatures.

BAY SCALLOP   3 in.

Another table delicacy, the Bay Scallop can
be found at the surface of the mud. Its
major defense against would-be predators is
to snap its shell shut, forcing a jet of water
that sends it randomly spinning away in the
water. The *reddish brown "scalloped" shell*,
when opened during feeding, reveals the
many *deep blue eyes* of the creature within.
Bay Scallops can occur in dense colonies in
shallow estuarine waters.

GEM SHELL

BALTIC
MACOMA

STOUT
TAGELUS

BAY
SCALLOP

Segmented Worms

Mudflats abound with the burrows of worms. Most marine worm species are segmented. Many kinds live in tubes, catching food that washes in or that they find on the surface. Others leave their burrows and swim freely in search of prey. You can find worms by scooping up a shovelful of mud. Put it into a strainer and swish the strainer in the water until you've washed all the mud off the worms.

CLAM WORM   8 in.

This common worm is *shiny green* with shades of brown and red. It swims well using the *fleshy paddles* on each body segment. The mouthparts, including sharp jaws, are normally contracted (like the head of a turtle in its shell) but can be pushed out to catch prey. Clam worms are aggressive predators and feed on many kinds of invertebrates, including other clam worms.

BLOOD WORM   To 15 in.

Well named, this rusty-green worm, which is commonly used to bait fish hooks, has *bright red blood.* Blood worms have a very long, muscular snout armed with *four small hooks* that they can shoot foward to capture prey. They can nip a finger, so be careful when handling them.

PLUMED WORM   12 in.

This worm builds a tube that projects a few inches above the mud surface and can go to 3 feet deep! The tube is made of leathery material embedded with tiny bits of shell. The worm itself is *iridescent greenish* with *bright red gill tufts.*

LUGWORM   8 in.

Lugworms build U-shaped burrows that are open at both ends. Look for the two holes. The 8-inch inhabitant is easily identified by its *robust shape* and *red gill tufts.* Lugworms are thickest toward the front. They eat mud and remove organic matter from it, much the same way earthworms do in soil.

CLAM WORM

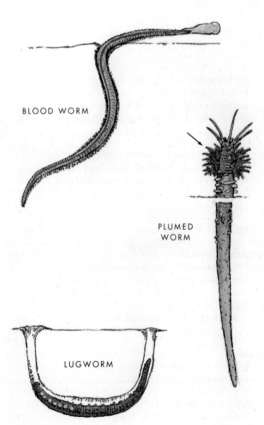

BLOOD WORM

PLUMED
WORM

LUGWORM

TEREBELLID WORM **To 18 in.**

This burrowing worm has a *dense tuft of soft tentacles* on its head. It builds a short mud tube in a burrow and collects organic matter by sweeping the mud surface with its tentacles. The worm's body is grayish yellow, the tentacles are tan, and there is a tuft of red gills near the mouth. The several species of terebellid worms are closely similar.

FRINGED WORM **From ½ to 10 in.**

The several different species of fringed worms of our coastal areas look alike, except for size. All have *long tentacles along their sides*, used to sweep the surface for food. Their long pinkish tentacles and red gills are delicate and easily broken.

FAN WORM **From less than ½ to 8 in.**

Like fringed worms, there are several common and similar species of fan worms, all of which live in leathery tubes covered with mud and sand. Some fan worms are quite tiny; others can grow to 8 inches. Only their heads protrude from their tubes, showing *two large fanned tufts* that sweep the water for food particles. They do not burrow but attach their tubes to rocks, shells, and other solid objects.

BAMBOO WORM **From less than ½ to 12 in.**

Bamboo worms are named for the arrangement of their segments, which *resembles the stem of a bamboo plant.* Color is usually grayish white with red where the segments join. These long, thin, easily damaged worms live in tubes in the mud.

PARCHMENT WORM **10 in.**

This odd-looking worm has perhaps the most unusual body structure of any segmented worm. The worm inhabits a parchment U-shaped tube that protrudes above the mud on both ends. The worm uses its *flimsy body paddles* to move water through the tube, removing food and oxygen from the water.

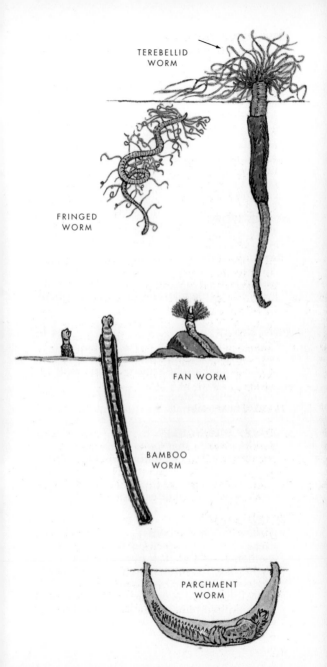

TEREBELLID
WORM

FRINGED
WORM

FAN WORM

BAMBOO
WORM

PARCHMENT
WORM

More Worms and Wormlike Animals

The long slender body shape of a worm is efficient for burrowing. This shape has helped other creatures adapt to life in the sea.

MILKY RIBBON WORM   To 4 ft.

This slender, *unsegmented* worm can reach astonishing lengths. Its *pink body* is *flattened*, and it is a graceful swimmer. Active mostly at night, the worm has a *long, pointed proboscis* that it uses as a spear to capture prey.

ACORN WORM   6 in.

Named for the resemblance of their front ends to an acorn, these worms have a *reddish collar* and a pointed pink snout that can be pushed out well beyond the collar or pulled in tightly. They live in burrows and feed on organic material collected in mucus that they produce.

PINK SYNAPTA   4 in.

Though it looks like a worm, this is a burrowing sea cucumber with a long, *pink-red* body and a *white ring of tentacles*. It normally hides in a hole or under a rock, with only its tentacles waving in search of food. These animals are quite fragile.

GOULD'S SIPUNCULID   12 in.

Here is a worm that looks like a sea cucumber. Gould's Sipunculids have *thick bodies,* usually golden brown in color, with a tentacle ring around their mouth that can be either retracted or extended.

ATHENARIAN   From less than 1
BURROWING ANEMONE   to 6 in.

There are several species of these burrowing anemones, and all look rather wormlike. Most species are *transparent* or *pink*. The *single ring* of tentacles is extended only when the animal is feeding: otherwise the entire animal remains tucked safely in its burrow.

MILKY
RIBBON WORM

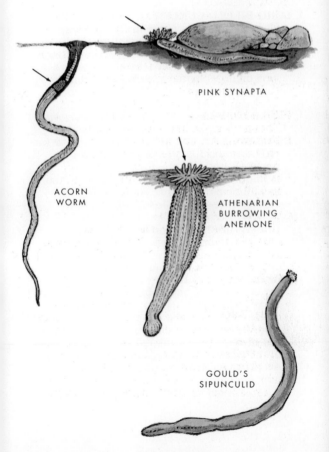

PINK SYNAPTA

ACORN
WORM

ATHENARIAN
BURROWING
ANEMONE

GOULD'S
SIPUNCULID

Mudflat Birds

Many shorebirds feed on the rich abundance of worms and mollusks that burrow in mudflats. Each species has a bill specialized to probe at a certain depth into the mud.

LONG-BILLED DOWITCHER   11–12 in.

A dowitcher has a *long, straight bill* that can reach deeply in search of burrowed worms. It feeds by rapidly probing up and down in the mud. In breeding plumage, the dowitcher is mostly orange-red. When it returns from its Arctic breeding grounds, it is mostly gray.

LONG-BILLED CURLEW   20–26 in.

One of the largest shorebirds, the Long-billed Curlew is most common along the Gulf Coast and in the West. It has an 8-inch *sickle-shaped bill* that acts as a sensitive forceps, locating even the deepest worms. Tan in color, when the bird flies it shows warm brownish red under its wings. Its name comes from its call, a whistled *cur-lee*.

DUNLIN   8–9 in.

This shorebird is often present in large flocks on both coasts during winter. A Dunlin resembles a small curlew as it, too, has a *down-curved bill*. With small bodies and short legs, Dunlins can reach only worms near the surface. In summer, Dunlins are *reddish* on the back with a *black patch* on the belly. They are dull gray in winter. Dunlins nest in the Arctic tundra.

AMERICAN AVOCET   16–20 in.

Avocets are large shorebirds with a bill that curves upward. This sharply patterned black and white bird has an *orangy* neck in breeding season. It does not probe in mud but instead sweeps its bill from side to side in the water, capturing small organisms. Avocets are most abundant in the West, breeding along inland marshes. They visit coastal areas mostly in winter.

LONG-BILLED
DOWITCHER

LONG-BILLED
CURLEW

DUNLIN

AMERICAN
AVOCET

Oyster Bars

COMMON OYSTER   **10 in.**

A bivalve with two differently shaped shells. The *upper shell is flat,* the *lower cup-shaped.* Oysters feed on tiny plankton that they filter from the water. Oysters form dense aggregations called bars.

Because oysters do not burrow or swim, many other animals settle on them. In fact, an entire ecological community depends upon the oyster. The **Sand-builder Worm**, about 1 inch long, builds a curved, brownish tube of cemented sand grains on oyster shells. The worm lives inside the tube. When it feeds, it pokes out its head, which is covered with *bright golden bristles.* Several species of **Hard Tube Worms,** the largest of which is just 3 inches long, build *little white tubes,* some shaped like a ram's horn. Like Sand-builder Worms, these worms also filter-feed. Scaled worms, including the 3-inch **Fifteen-scaled Worm** shown here, are flattened, with *platelike scales.* They can cling tightly to any surface.

Several species of **Mud Crabs** live among the oysters. Each is about an inch and a half long, *brown* with *black tips on its claws.* The tiny **Oyster Crab**, barely half an inch long, lives inside the oyster itself. It has a *round shell.* A single oyster may harbor over 100 of these crabs. The crabs take some of the oyster's food and are protected inside the shells.

The **Oyster Drill,** about an inch long, is a *small white snail* that is a major oyster predator. It drills into the animal and devours it. Another oyster threat is the **Boring Sponge.** It has a *yellow, spreading shape,* and can overgrow the oyster's shell, killing the animal within.

Yet another resident of the oyster bar, the **Big-clawed Snapping Shrimp,** is about 2 inches long. Its *large claw* makes a popping sound.

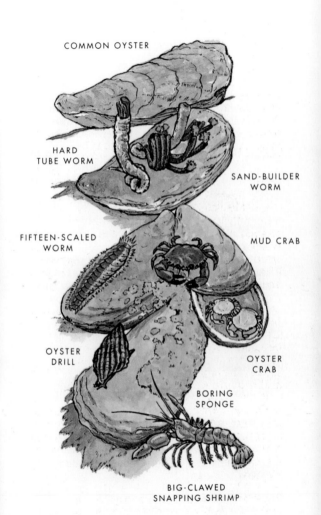

COMMON OYSTER

HARD
TUBE WORM

SAND-BUILDER
WORM

FIFTEEN-SCALED
WORM

MUD CRAB

OYSTER
DRILL

OYSTER
CRAB

BORING
SPONGE

BIG-CLAWED
SNAPPING SHRIMP

Eelgrass flats

EELGRASS   3 ft.
Eelgrass is a marine plant related to fresh-
water pondweeds. Its *long green blades* grow
in shallow protected areas near salt
marshes. Many animal species live among
the underwater meadows of Eelgrass.

PIPEFISH   4–12 in.
A very *slender* fish, brownish green with
yellow on the belly, but can change color to
blend with its background. Often spotted.
Note *long, pointed snout.* Several species.

LINED SEAHORSE   6 in.
Unmistakable. *Horselike head,* with long
snout, upright posture, curled tail. Most are
light yellow-brown, with white speckles.
Pipefish and Seahorses are closely related.
Males brood the babies in a unique pouch
on the male's abdomen.

THREESPINE STICKLEBACK   4 in.
Sticklebacks are named for their sharp
spines. This species has *three spines* near
its top fin, two large and one small (in front
of the fin). Color is greenish brown above
and silvery on the sides. During breeding
season males have *red bellies* and *blue eyes.*
Stickleback males guard nests made of
vegetation stuck together with mucus.

EELGRASS SACOGLOSSAN SLUG   ½ in.
A *green* nudibranch common to Eelgrass
meadows but hard to find, as it so well
camouflaged.

SEA PILL BUG   ½ in.
Pill bugs are crustaceans called isopods that
roll into a ball when disturbed. There are
many marine species. This one is *rounded,*
with a *wide tail.*

SLENDER ISOPOD   1 in.
An isopod with a *wormlike* shape.

SLENDER TUBE-MAKER   To ½ in.
Slender amphipods that build tubes of mud,
sand, and debris, and live in dense colonies.

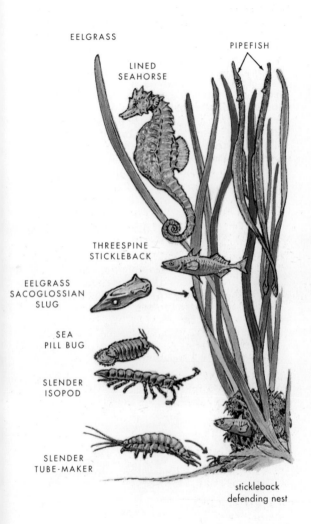

EELGRASS

PIPEFISH

LINED
SEAHORSE

THREESPINE
STICKLEBACK

EELGRASS
SACOGLOSSIAN
SLUG

SEA
PILL BUG

SLENDER
ISOPOD

SLENDER
TUBE-MAKER

stickleback
defending nest

Salt Marshes and Estuaries

Coastal salt marshes are invaluable resources that provide food and habitat for countless plants and animals. Nearest the sea, where grasses are usually immersed in saltwater, is a zone of **Salt Marsh Cord Grass.** This grass can top 8 feet tall. Behind this grows a zone of **Salt Meadow Cord Grass,** a shorter grass that grows as a tousled, cowlicked mat. Several species of **Glasswort** grow among the cord grasses, often forming dense mats. Glassworts have thick stems and turn bright orange-red in fall. Farther from the sea you'll find **Common Reed,** a tall yellowish grass with large brown seed tufts.

OSPREY

SALT MARSH
CORD GRASS

WILLET

GLASSWORT

CLAPPER
RAIL

SALT MEADOW
CORD GRASS

Salt marshes abound with birds. Listen for the sharp whistles of an **Osprey**, or fish hawk, as it plunges talons-first into the water. The shaggy-crested **Belted Kingfisher** dives head-first for fish. Females have a reddish belly band. The **Willet** is a large, grayish sandpiper with bold black and white patterning under its wings and a loud whistled *pill-will-willet* call. The **Clapper Rail**, a chicken-sized bird, is adept at slinking unseen among the grasses.

Salt marsh tide pools provide fish for the all-white **American Egret** and slate blue **Little Blue Heron.** At night these same pools are visited by hungry **Black-crowned Night Herons.** These chunky waders utter a distinctive *"quok!"* as they fly over.

BELTED
KINGFISHER

COMMON
REED

BLACK-CROWNED
NIGHT HERON

LITTLE BLUE
HERON

AMERICAN
EGRET

Small Creatures of the Salt Marsh

RIBBED MUSSEL   4 in.
This common bivalve lives in large colonies among the stems of the cord grass. It is named for the *ridges* that run along the shells. Mussels constantly filter nutrients from the water, which are then deposited in the mussels' droppings. This "fertilizer" enhances the growth of marsh plants.

ANGEL WING   7 in.
A large *white shell,* quite brittle and often found broken. Shell feels rough because of the *scaly ribs. Raised hinge* is distinctive. Angel Wings burrow in thick peat and clay in salt marshes, and are filter-feeders.

FALSE ANGEL WING   2 in.
Like the Angel Wing but smaller, with a smaller, less raised hinge. Shaped like sharpened wedges, both Angel Wings and False Angel Wings can quickly burrow through thick peat. Like Angel Wings, False Angel Wing shells are fragile, and broken pieces are common on beaches.

SALT MARSH SNAIL $1/2$ in.
This small snail with a *banded shell* is often abundant, grazing on stalks of cord grass.

GRASS SHRIMP   Less than 1 in.
A small shrimp that can be very abundant in tidal channels. These small creatures can be either *shiny green* or *translucent brown.* They are easy to watch as they congregate around a dead fish or other food.

MUD DOG WHELK   1 in.
Hundreds of these little snails will gather at fish carcasses, and their trails are readily visible in the mud. Shells are *smooth* and *dark brown,* like the mud they inhabit.

GREENHEAD FLY $1/2$ in.
This insect is one of the most obvious and irritating marsh animals. A nuisance to people because of its painful bite, this husky fly has *large green eyes.* You need not look for it— it will find you.

RIBBED MUSSELS

GREENHEAD FLY

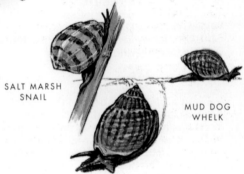

SALT MARSH
SNAIL

MUD DOG
WHELK

GRASS SHRIMP

ANGEL WING

FALSE
ANGEL WING

Salt Marsh Fishes

MUMMICHOG   5 in.

The Mummichog has a single dorsal fin and a rather *blunt head*. Males in breeding condition are bluish black above with a *bright yellow belly*. Females are olive, with paler fins. Both sexes have a *rounded tail*.

STRIPED KILLIFISH   7 in.

Similar to a Mummichog but with a more *pointed snout*. Males have vertical black stripes, and females have horizontal stripes. Breeding males have bright *orange bellies*. Killifishes and Mummichogs are abundant in salt marsh channels and pools. Both are often called minnows and are used for bait. They are small but ecologically valuable, as they feed heavily on mosquito larvae.

TIDEWATER SILVERSIDE   6 in.

Siversides are *slender* fish with bright *silvery* bodies. They often occur in schools with killifishes, feeding on tiny shrimps, worms, larvae, and fish eggs.

AMERICAN SHAD   20 in.

Also a silvery fish, with a *deeply forked tail fin* and a *black spot* behind the gills. In spring, American Shad migrate through salt marshes to fresh water in order to spawn. Their eggs, called shad roe, are a popular seasonal delicacy. Shad spend the winter months in the ocean.

AMERICAN EEL   3 ft.

Elongated shape, greenish, with *long dorsal fin*. Like shad, American Eels also migrate from the ocean to fresh water but not to breed. All eels breed in the tropical Sargasso Sea in the south Atlantic. The young eels, called glass eels or elvers, migrate upstream by night, burrowing under stones to rest during the day. They remain in estuaries and rivers until sexually mature (at about 3 feet in length). At that time they return to the Sargasso Sea to breed.

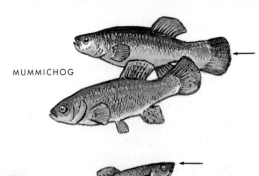

MUMMICHOG

STRIPED
KILLIFISH

TIDEWATER
SILVERSIDE

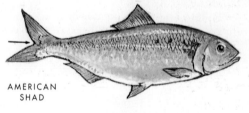

AMERICAN
SHAD

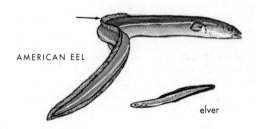

AMERICAN EEL

elver

Salt Marsh Plants

Though grasses and glassworts are the most common salt marsh plants, many other less abundant plants are worth looking for among the grasses.

SEA LAVENDER   12–24 in.

Also called Marsh Rosemary, Sea Lavender has *large unlobed leaves* that hug the ground. From midsummer to early fall, the *many-branched, spreading stalk* is lined with delicate *light purple flowers*. Sea Lavender is often used in dried floral arrangements.

SALT-MARSH FLEABANE   8–36 in.

A member of the huge family that includes daisies, asters, and goldenrods, this common salt marsh plant blossoms in late summer. It has flattened, *brushlike*, purple-pink flower heads. Leaves alternate on either side of the stem and are slightly notched. Salt Marsh Fleabane smells somewhat like camphor and is sticky to the touch.

PERENNIAL   12–24 in.
SALT-MARSH ASTER

This plant has *daisylike* flower heads that may be either white or pink. Leaves are *very slender*. A similar species, Annual Salt Marsh Aster, has slightly wider leaves and smaller flower heads.

SEASIDE GERARDIA   12 in.

This is a *slender-leaved* plant with rosy-purple *trumpet-shaped* flowers that bloom from midsummer through early autumn. Leaves feel spongy, like glasswort leaves. Bees are very attracted to the flowers of Seaside Gerardia.

SEA
LAVENDER

SALT-MARSH
FLEABANE

PERENNIAL
SALT-MARSH
ASTER

SEASIDE
GERARDIA

MARSH ELDER   3 ft.

Marsh Elder is a salt marsh shrub. It is
identified by its shrubby shape and *spikes*
of *greenish white flowers* that bloom from
late summer through fall. Note that the
leaves of Marsh Elder are *opposite*, meaning
that leaves always emerge in pairs on opposite sides of the stem. Most plants, such as
the asters, for example, have *alternate*
leaves that do not grow opposite each other.
Marsh Elder leaves are long and have
notches, or teeth, along their edge

GROUNDSEL-TREE   5–6 ft.

Groundsel-tree is a species in which each
tree is either male or female, and the two
sexes have different flowers. Male flowers
have *white "bristles"* that the *yellowish
white* female flowers lack. Leaves are *thick*,
with few teeth. Flowers bloom from late
summer through fall and are pollinated by
the brisk winds blowing across the marsh.
Pollen from the male flowers is blown
around, and some of it reaches the female
flowers on other plants. Because male and
female flowers are on separate plants, a
single plant cannot reproduce. Groundsel-
trees are often common in higher areas in
salt marshes, forming a dense, shrubby
zone.

BLUE-EYED GRASS   To 24 in.

Though it looks very much like a typical
grass, Blue-eyed Grass is actually an iris, a
member of the lily family. The leaf blades
resemble grass, but the flower, *blue-violet
with a yellow center*, reveals the plant's true
identity. Flowers bloom from mid-spring
though summer.

MARSH
ELDER

GROUNDSEL-TREE

BLUE-EYED
GRASS

Land Birds of the Salt Marsh

RED-WINGED BLACKBIRD   **7–9½ in.**

This unmistakable bird is among the most common marsh birds. Red-wings are often abundant. The *glossy black* males display their *bright red wing patches* as they perch atop the grasses and sing an energetic *ee-oh-lay*. Females are smaller, with brown streaks, and resemble large sparrows. Females build nests tucked carefully among the salt marsh grasses. Red-winged Blackbird males use their bright red wing patches, called epaulettes, to help them claim their territories in the marsh. Other males take notice of the red "badges" of ownership. Often one male will have several females nesting within his territory. Females are more secretive, skulking among the marsh grasses, ever on the lookout for raccoons, rats, or other potential nest predators. Young male Red-wings look very much like females.

TREE SWALLOW   **5–6 in.**

Tree Swallows skim the marsh in pursuit of mosquitoes and other insect prey. Both sexes look the same: *iridescent greenish blue* above, bright white below. These swallows nest in hollow trees, so they frequently nest some distance from their feeding places in the marshes. Occasionally, a female will lay her egg in another female's nest when the other bird is away. Tree Swallows take readily to bird boxes and should be welcomed because they eat large numbers of flying insects. In late summer, Tree Swallows gather, often in flocks of a thousand or more, to feed on insects and bayberries, which will become their fuel for their long migration.

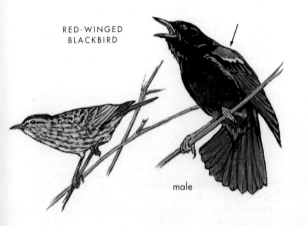

RED-WINGED
BLACKBIRD

male

TREE
SWALLOW

MARSH WREN   5 in.

Marsh Wrens sing their gurgling songs from cord grass stalks. Wrens are quite small, and both sexes are reddish brown with a *white eyestripe* and *white streaking* on the back. Male Marsh Wrens build many "dummy nests" in an attempt to attract females to their territories. Once a female selects a territory in which to nest, she usually builds her own nest, in spite of the efforts of the resident male.

Two sparrows, the Sharp-tailed Sparrow and the Seaside Sparrow, make their nests in the salt marshes. They skulk around in the grasses and are best seen when they are singing atop a grass stalk. It takes patience and perseverence to see them well.

SHARP-TAILED SPARROW   5 in.

A *chunky* sparrow with a buffy breast and *streaking* on the breast and back. The face has a *triangle* of yellowish orange striping around the eyes. The tail is short and pointed. Song is a weak trilling, not very musical.

SEASIDE SPARROW   5½ in.

Dark brown with fairly *heavy streaking* on the breast. At close range, look for a *small patch of yellow* in front of the eye. Its tail is pointed, like the Sharp-tail's, but longer. Its song sounds somewhat like that of the Red-winged Blackbird, but fainter.

AMERICAN OYSTERCATCHER   17–21 in.

The American Oystercatcher is often seen on mudflats at low tide as it adeptly opens bivalve shells and eats their inhabitants. It is a large bird, brown and white with a *black head* and long *bright red bill.* This shorebird is currently extending its range northward. Listen for its loud *wheep* call.

MARSH
WREN

SHARP-TAILED
SPARROW

SEASIDE
SPARROW

AMERICAN
OYSTERCATCHER

Birdlife in an Estuary

An estuary or bay is the place where fresh water rivers meet salt water from the ocean. Rich in food washed in from salt marshes by the rivers, estuaries are used as nurseries by many fish and other marine animals. This attracts many different kinds of birds.

BLACK SKIMMER   16–20 in.

A *sharply patterned* bird, black above and white below, with slender *pointed wings.* The lower half of its black and red bill is much *longer* than the upper half, and the bird skims over the water of the bay, scooping up tiny animals in its open bill.

BROWN PELICAN   50 in.

Unmistakable. Pelicans are large birds with an almost prehistoric look to them. They are dark brown with a *long, baglike bill.* Brown Pelicans may soar high above the water or glide almost effortlessly above the waves. The Brown Pelican dives for fish, crashing head first into the water. Brown Pelicans are common along the southeastern, Gulf, and Pacific coasts. In recent years they have been found as far north as New Jersey and New York.

RED-BREASTED MERGANSER   20–26 in.

This colorful duck sits on the water and dives for fish. Mergansers have bills lined with teeth-like serrations, an aid in holding slippery fish. Males have *red bills* and *green heads*; females are *grayish* with *reddish heads.* Red-breasted Mergansers winter in estuaries and along seacoasts, but they breed on northern inland lakes, where they nest in tree cavities.

SURF SCOTER   19 in.

Scoters are husky ducks that dive to feed on clams and mussels. This species is common on both coasts. Males are *black* with *white patches* on the head and *bright orange-red* on the bill. Females are brown. In winter, large numbers of scoters flock together in estuaries and the open sea.

BLACK
SKIMMER

BROWN
PELICAN

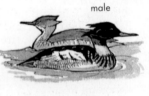

male

RED-BREASTED
MERGANSER

male

SURF
SCOTER

Some Estuarine Fish

WHITE PERCH   **19 in.**

One of many fish that spawn in estuaries during the spring and summer. This silvery, basslike fish is flattened from side to side, and has a *rounded upper back.* Its tail is *not* deeply forked.

SHEEPSHEAD   **3 ft.**

Sheepshead belong to the porgy family, whose members generally have a high forehead and a single fin on their back, spiny in the front. This species has *5–6 vertical black bands* along its sides. Sheepshead are popular game fish and tasty eating. A big one can weigh 20 pounds. They are common in southeastern and Gulf waters.

NORTHERN SEAROBIN   **15 in.**

A bottom-dwelling fish that "walks" about on the *long rays* of its *wing-shaped fins* in search of crabs, mollusks, and worms. Note the large head and long snout.

HOGCHOKER   **8 in.**

This oddly named fish is one of several flatfish, the flounders and soles, that inhabit estuaries. Its small size and *oval shape* make it easy to identify. In spite of its unappetizing name, this little fish is closely related to the famous European sole, and is delicious to eat.

BLUNTNOSE STINGRAY   **3 ft.**

Stingrays are also flattened but are related to sharks, not flounders. They have *winglike fins* and long, *whip-shaped tails.* Stingrays glide over the bottom in search of food. Beware of stepping on or handling stingrays: a sharp spine at the base of the tail can inflict a very painful wound.

SANDBAR SHARK   **To 10 ft.**

This is one of several shark species to enter estuaries. All sharks have a *pointed snout* and *exposed gills,* visible along their sides. Young Sandbar Sharks feed on crabs and fish as they mature in the estuary.

WHITE
PERCH

SHEEPSHEAD

NORTHERN
SEAROBIN

HOGCHOKER

BLUNTNOSE
STINGRAY

SANDBAR
SHARK

Tiny Plants and Animals

Like the word *planet*, *plankton* comes from the Greek root meaning "wanderer." Tiny plants and animals, many too small to be seen with your eye alone, float in ocean waters, mostly at the mercy of the currents. Some larger animals are planktonic in their larval stages. Plant plankton form an important base in the oceanic food chain. You can catch plankton by waving a fine-mesh net back and forth under the water. Examine the resulting slime with a microscope or hand lens.

Diatoms are microscopic one-celled plants that live in *tiny "glass" shells* made of silica. They are generally golden brown and may be *disc* or *needle-shaped*, or linked together in chains. **Dinoflagellates** are one-celled animals that tend to be golden brown. They propel themselves weakly with *whiplike flagella*. Some are *reddish* and produce a potentially dangerous poison known as red tide. **Foraminiferans** and **Radiolarians** are tiny one-celled animals related to amoebas. Foraminiferans make chalky shells that resemble tiny snails. Radiolarians inhabit "glass" shells, some of which have long spines.

Copepods are tiny crustaceans, the largest of which is about the size of a grain of rice. With their *long antennae* propelling them, they swim with a *jerky* motion. Most are transparent bluish white with a *red pigment spot*.

Comb Jellies are not jellyfish but belong to a separate group that does not sting. Out of water, they look like shapeless blobs and are quite fragile. They emit their own light, like fireflies, and can make a bay glow in the dark. They are iridescent blue, red, and violet.

COMMON NORTHERN COMB JELLY   **6 in.**
   Bell shaped, very common on the New England coast in summer.

SEA GOOSEBERRY   **1 in.**
   Rounded, with *long tentacles*. Like other comb jellies, it is a voracious and even cannibalistic predator, usually feeding on fish eggs and larvae.

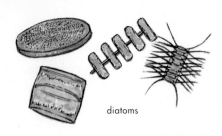

diatoms

dinoflagellates

foraminiferans

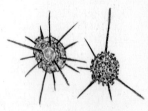

radiolarians

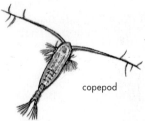

copepod

COMMON NORTHERN
COMB JELLY

SEA
GOOSEBERRY

These planktonic animals are large enough to be seen without a microscope, but a magnifying glass will help you see details.

ARROW WORMS   Less than 1 in.
Named for their streamlined shape, these are tiny, almost transparent, predators. They attack larval fish and anything else they can capture. They often become abundant in estuaries. Note the *paired fins, fishlike tail,* and *bristles* around the mouth.

MYSID SHRIMP   1 in.
Mysid shrimp inhabit estuaries by the millions. They spend the day on the bottom, but, like many tiny animal plankton, they swim to the surface at night to feed. They are quite *slender* with a more wormlike body than other shrimp.

HORNED KRILL   1 in.
These tiny *pink* shrimp can occur in such vast numbers that the seawater is sometimes colored pink by them. They look very much like mysid shrimp but occur in the open ocean, not in estuaries. Krill are an important food for many seabirds and for whales, which consume krill by the billions.

CRAB LARVAE
All crabs lay eggs, which hatch into tiny larvae that are temporary members of the plankton. A typical crab larva goes through several different stages. The first stage, which resembles a tiny mite, is called a nauplius. It gradually grows and changes into a zoea, with *long head spines.* The zoea then changes to a megalops, which has *prominent claws* that make the animal begin to look more like a crab.

NAKED SEA BUTTERFLY   1 in.
This somewhat transparent, reddish creature is a tiny planktonic snail without a shell. It uses its *winglike feet* to help it move weakly through the sea in search of plant plankton.

ARROW
WORMS

MYSID SHRIMP

HORNED KRILL

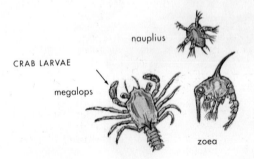

nauplius

CRAB LARVAE

megalops

zoea

NAKED SEA
BUTTERFLY

Dunes and Barrier Beaches

The forces of tides, waves, and currents pile up sand in vast beaches and large dunes. A barrier beach is a long strip of dunes along the coastline that protects estuaries and salt marshes from the ravages of the sea. Unstable sand, salt spray, and drying winds all pose problems to which dune plants have adapted. The most hardy plants are found on the *foredunes*, the area nearest the sea. The *interdunes* are more protected, and the *backdunes* are relatively well protected from sea spray.

Foredune plants include **Beach Grass, Sea-rocket,** and **Dusty Miller.** Beach Grass blades can curl up to keep their water from evaporating. Sea-rocket has thick leaves and pale lavender flowers. Dusty Miller, related to the

YELLOW-RUMPED WARBLER

BAYBERRY

MONARCH

BEACH HEATHER

SEASIDE GOLDENROD

SALT SPRAY ROSE

sagebrush of western deserts, has pale leaves covered by tiny white hairs and yellow flowers.

Beach Pea and **Salt Spray Rose** may be found on the foredunes and interdunes. Beach Pea, with rosy purple flowers, is a vine, its tendrils curling around other plants. Salt Spray Rose is a dense shrub with white or pink-red flowers. The fruits, called rose hips, are red. **Seaside Goldenrod** is common along the coast. Its thick leaves protect it from water loss and salt damage. Migrating **Monarch butterflies** feed on nectar from its bright yellow blossoms. **Beach Heather** is a low-growing, grayish green plant with small yellow flowers. **Bayberry**, a common shrub of interdunes and backdunes, has aromatic greenish blue berries attract migrating **Yellow-rumped Warblers,** named for their bright rump patch.

BEACH PEA

SEA-ROCKET

DUSTY MILLER

BEACH GRASS

Southeastern Dune Trees

The beachcomber who walks the sands of the Florida and Gulf coasts, as well as the Caribbean, will encounter plants not found in more northern climates.

SEA GRAPE   To 20 ft.

Sea Grape is a small, spreading tree, easily recognized by its *large* (to 11 in.), leathery, oval leaves with red veins. It produces clusters of edible "grapes" that are *green* when young and turn *purple* when ripe. Sea Grape is a tropical species found in Florida and throughout the Caribbean.

COCONUT PALM   To 60 ft.

This graceful, gray-barked tree produces *football-sized* brown fruits called husks, which are green when young and gradually turn brown. Inside is the delicious edible nut. The coconuts are in clusters beneath the crown of *fanlike leaves.* Coconut Palms are found worldwide throughout the tropics.

MANCHINEEL   To 30 ft.

Manchineel is a tree to be avoided, especially in wet weather. The *oval-shaped leaves,* as well as the twigs and bark, drip poison when it rains. The apple-like, *greenish yellow fruit* is also poisonous. Look at Manchineel from a safe distance.

SEASIDE MAHO   To 30 ft.

Seaside Maho is a small spreading tree or shrub with *shiny heart-shaped leaves.* The large flowers are *yellow* with *violet centers.* This tropical species grows on beaches in Florida and throughout the West Indies.

SPANISH BAYONET   To 25 ft.

Also called Yucca, this plant is easily identified by its *rosette* of *thick, swordlike, sharply pointed leaves.* The *white bell-shaped flowers* grow in a dense cluster atop a long central stalk. Yuccas live scattered among other plants on southern dunes.

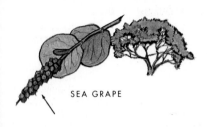

SEA GRAPE

COCONUT PALM

MANCHINEEL

SEASIDE MAHO

SPANISH BAYONET

Birds of the Dunes

PEREGRINE FALCON   15–20 in.

Dunewalkers looking skyward in the fall
might sight a migrating Peregrine Falcon.
This magnificent bird of prey, like the
Osprey and the Brown Pelican, was seri-
ously endangered by pesticides. Since the
use of the pesticide DDT was banned, the
Peregrine population is now growing well,
and it has been successfully reintroduced in
many of its old homes. Most Peregrines nest
in arctic and subarctic regions, but some
nest in cities and feed on pigeons. Peregrines have *sharply pointed wings* and are
nearly crow-sized. They have a *black crescent* on their face. The sexes look alike, but
males are somewhat smaller than females.
Young birds are as large as adults, but are
brown rather than *slate blue.* Peregrines
attack flying ducks and shorebirds,
plunging from high above in a dive that can
exceed 100 miles per hour.

SNOWY OWL   20–27 in.

Snowy Owls, the large white owls of the
Arctic, don't seem to mind the most severe
winter cold and icy winds. But they sometimes move south in winter, when the
supply of lemmings, a small rodent that is
their normal food, is too low. Though some
birds remain inland, most seem to like the
coastal beaches and dunes, sometimes
reaching as far south as the Carolinas. All
Snowy Owls are *white,* but female and
young birds are *heavily barred* with brown
and black. Adult males are almost pure
white. Their eyes are *blazing yellow.* As in
Peregrines, females are slightly larger than
males. Snowy Owls often hunt by day and
tend to perch in the open, often atop a high
dune, where the owl can survey a wide area
as it looks for prey.

PEREGRINE FALCON

SNOWY OWL

HORNED LARK   8 in.

A small bird, reddish brown above, pale below, with a *black neck* and yellowish face marked by a *black crescent.* Look for their tiny "horns," which are really feathers. When the bird is overhead, you can see the *black tail* with *white outer feathers.* Some Horned Larks nest along seashores, but many nest in interior regions and in the far north. In winter, large flocks move to coastal regions, surviving on food found among the dune plants. On the ground, they always *walk*, never hop like sparrows. The Horned Lark is a ground bird of open areas and virtually never perches in trees. It has a long, tinkling, melodious song, often given when the bird is high overhead. The nest is well concealed among grasses.

SNOW BUNTING   7 in.

Snow Buntings look like robust sparrows, but appear nearly *all white* when in flight. When seen walking atop the dunes, they reveal the rich *reddish markings* on their back. They are birds of the far north, nesting well above the treeline in the Arctic. In summer the males become black and white, but in winter, when they normally are seen in the United States, males resemble the brownish females. Snow Buntings migrate in large flocks, often of 100 or more birds. They don't seem to mind a raging snowstorm, and resemble snowflakes as they fly through the blizzard.

LAPLAND LONGSPUR   6½ in.

Longspurs are similar in size to Horned Larks and Snow Buntings. Like the buntings, they nest in the far north, where caribou and Polar Bears reside. They look like sparrows, with blackish brown streaks and *chestnut collars.* They are named for their long hind claw. Longspurs often are found among Snow Bunting and Horned Lark flocks, scampering across the dunes in search of seeds.

HORNED LARK

SNOW BUNTING

LAPLAND
LONGSPUR

The Open Ocean

Sargassum Weed Community

The Sargasso Sea is a vast area of the tropical southwestern Atlantic Ocean. A unique type of alga, called Sargassum Weed, gives the sea its name and provides the basis for an entire community of animals. Look for Sargassum Weed washed up on southern beaches and see what tiny creatures it may shelter.

SARGASSUM WEED   24 in. or longer
This brown alga, often called Gulfweed, has *narrow fronds* containing many *small gas bladders,* like tiny grapes. Some forms attach to rocks and ships, and others are free-floating.

SARGASSUM FROGFISH   4–8 in.
This fish not only lives in Sargassum Weed, it even looks like Sargassum Weed. It has a *large fleshy spine* atop its head and a *smaller spine between its eyes.* These spines act as lures to bring smaller fish within reach of the frogfish's large mouth.

SARGASSUM PIPEFISH   8 in.
Also well camouflaged in its Sargassum Weed home, this pipefish is yellowish green with *red bands* around its underside.

SARGASSUM SWIMMING CRAB   1 in.
A swimming crab, with *paddles* on its rear legs. If separated from its shelter, it will quickly return. The crab's shell is almost exactly the color of the weed, making it very difficult to spot.

SARGASSUM SEA SLUG   3½ in.
This sea slug is also amazingly well camouflaged. Its *leglike fleshy paddles* help it remain secure in the Sargassum Weed.

OCEANIC TWO-WING FLYINGFISH   10 in.
Flyingfish are silvery, with *huge fins* that look and act like wings. Flyingfish do not actually fly, but leap from the sea and glide, sometimes up to 100 feet or more.

SARGASSUM
WEED

SARGASSUM
FROGFISH

SARGASSUM
PIPEFISH

SARGASSUM
SEA SLUG

SARGASUM
SWIMMING CRAB

OCEANIC
TWO-WING FLYINGFISH

Porpoises and Dolphins

While the names "porpoise" and "dolphin" are often confused, they signify different animals. Both are marine mammals, but porpoises have blunt snouts, and dolphins have pointed snouts. To further complicate matters, a colorful game fish is also called Dolphin. It is quite distinct from the mammals.

HARBOR PORPOISE 6 ft.

Harbor Porpoises are common from New England to Florida and along most of the Pacific Coast. Schools of up to 50 are often seen swimming near the shore. They are dark brown to bluish gray with pale *gray-white sides* and a pinkish belly. The snout is quite *blunt,* the top fin small and triangular. They eat small fish and squid.

WHITE-SIDED DOLPHIN 9 ft.

Two species, the Atlantic White-sided Dolphin and the Pacific White-sided Dolphin, look much alike. The Atlantic species is grayish black above with gray and white belly and sides and a *tan-yellow* streak near the tail. The Pacific species is grayish on the sides and upper fin with a pure white belly. Both species often associate with whales, and groups of several hundred to a thousand or more can occur.

BOTTLENOSE DOLPHIN 12 ft.

Like the White-sided Dolphin, there is an Atlantic and a Pacific species of bottlenose dolphin. Both prefer warm water, and both are intelligent. They are frequently exhibited doing tricks at aquariums and seaquariums. They have a *long snout* (the bottlenose) and are almost uniformly bluish brown, with white bellies.

DOLPHIN 5 ft.

Dolphins are streamlined game fish that are *deep blue above* and *brilliant yellow below,* with blue spots. The tail is yellow. Males have *high, rounded foreheads.* Dolphins can be found in tropical seas all over the world, where they feed on flyingfishes.

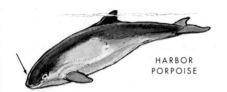

HARBOR
PORPOISE

WHITE-SIDED
DOLPHIN

BOTTLENOSE
DOLPHIN

DOLPHIN

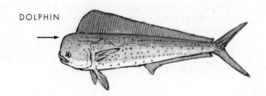

Mangrove Forests

Mangrove trees can withstand high levels of saltwater. Mangrove forests and islands line the south Florida coast and Keys and the Caribbean.

RED MANGROVE   To 40 ft.
This small, spreading tree has *reddish roots* that grow as conspicuous curved stilts, anchoring the tree in the shifting coral sand. Leaves are *waxy, shiny green.* Seedlings, called "sea pencils," look like long pods.

WOOD STORK   5 ft.
The only stork native to the United States. It is easily recognized by its large size and bold *black and white plumage.* The head is ashy gray with a *long downcurved bill.*

WHITE IBIS   2 ft.
The White Ibis is only about half the size of a Wood Stork and has *black only on its wingtips.* Its bill and legs are bright red. Ibis and Wood Storks use their long, curved bills to probe deeply into soft mud in search of various worms and other marine animals.

ROSEATE SPOONBILL   3 ft.
This unmistakable wading bird is named for its odd, greenish, *spoon-shaped bill,* which it sweeps through muddy water to scoop up small marine animals. The wings are *bright pink,* especially on the shoulders. Legs are red. Large colonies of spoonbills often nest in the mangroves.

MANATEE   7–13 ft.
This odd-looking mammal lives in channels among mangrove islands. With its *large fins* and *fishlike tail,* the Manatee is reputed to be the basis for mermaid legends— hard to believe considering its *doglike, whiskered face.* Manatees resemble seals but are not closely related to them, and they are strict vegetarians. Manatees are often injured in collisions with power boats and are much reduced in population. They are considered an endangered species.

RED MANGROVE

WOOD
STORK

WHITE
IBIS

ROSEATE
SPOONBILL

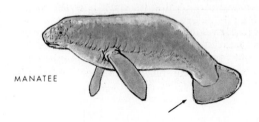

MANATEE

MAGNIFICENT FRIGATEBIRD   3½ ft.

Also called the Man-Of-War Bird, this graceful bird of tropical oceans is one of the world's finest fliers. Flocks are often seen soaring high overhead like kites. Note the *thin and and pointed wings*, which spread 7 feet across, and the *forked tail*. Frigatebirds are named for their habit of attacking gulls, terns, and pelicans, forcing them to drop fish, which the Frigatebirds catch and eat. Male Frigatebirds are *glossy black* and have huge *expandable red pouches* that hang like balloons from their throats and are used to attract females. Females are *white* on the breast, and lack the big throat pouches.

ANHINGA   3 ft.

Also called Water Turkey, this bird is a long-necked relative of cormorants. Males are black, with *much white* on the shoulders and upper wings and a *white tail band*. Females have *brown heads and necks*. Anhingas, like Frigatebirds, often are seen soaring high overhead. They feed on fish that they capture by diving from the surface of the water.

REDDISH EGRET   30 in.

This long-legged wader is found not only among the mangroves but along the Gulf Coast as well. It has a *slate blue* body with a *shaggy, reddish brown* neck and head. The bill is two-toned, black at the tip and *pink* at the base. Reddish Egrets "dance" when hunting fish. They spread their wings and prance around as they stalk their scaly prey.

YELLOW-CROWNED   24 in.
NIGHT HERON

A chunky gray heron with *bright yellow legs*. Its face is striped with black and white, and its forehead is pale yellow. Its eyes are bright red. Though night herons feed at night, they are often seen during the day roosting in the mangroves.

MAGNIFICENT
FRIGATEBIRD

ANHINGA

REDDISH
EGRET

YELLOW-CROWNED
NIGHT HERON

Mangrove Crabs and Snails

SOLDIER CRAB   1 1/2 in.
Also called the Common Land Hermit Crab.
It is frequently sighted tucked among the
mangrove roots. Like all hermit crabs, it
always carries a snail shell for shelter. One
of the two front claws is much larger than
the other. Claws, *orange below* and *purple
above*, can give a sharp pinch. These crabs
burrow deep in the sand and live out of
water, returning to the sea only to lay eggs.

CARIBBEAN MUD   Less than 1 in.
FIDDLER CRAB
There are many species of fiddler crabs, and
all live in large colonies not only among
mangroves but also in salt marshes all the
way to New England. Males of all species
have an extremely large claw that is used in
courting females and that gives the species
its name. Color ranges from tan to greenish.
The Caribbean Mud Fiddler Crab occurs
from Florida to Texas.

MANGROVE LAND CRAB   2 1/2 in.
This crab lives in burrows among the
mangroves from Florida to Brazil. Its shell is
deep purple with *yellow edges*. The *hairy*
legs are reddish, spotted with yellow. Eyes
are on *red stalks*.

SPOTTED MANGROVE CRAB   2 in.
This little crab climbs skillfully up mangrove
roots to eat leaves. It is greenish brown with
light spots on the shell, with reddish legs
spotted with yellow. Eyes are on *red stalks*.

MANGROVE PERIWINKLE   1 in.
This little snail is often abundant on
mangrove roots. It is tan with *bluish green
stripes* around the shell.

FLORIDA CROWN CONCH   8 in.
This large snail scavenges in mud between
mangrove roots. It has elaborate *brown and
tan stripes* and *rows of open spines*.

SOLDIER CRAB

CARIBBEAN MUD
FIDDLER CRAB

MANGROVE
LAND CRAB

SPOTTED
MANGROVE CRAB

MANGROVE
PERIWINKLE

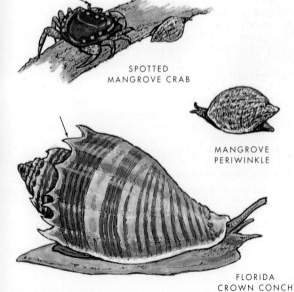

FLORIDA
CROWN CONCH

Animals of the Mangrove Roots

The long, slender roots of Red Mangroves serve as attachment sites for many small marine animals. Juvenile coral reef fish also lurk among the jungle of roots.

MANGROVE TUNICATE   1 in.

Clusters of baglike tunicates, like colorful bunches of grapes, attach to roots and filter the warm water, capturing tiny prey in their mucus-lined gills. Mangrove Tunicates are *club-shaped* and *orangy red.*

PAINTED TUNICATE   Less than 1 in.

This tunicate grows in *dense clusters* and is *pale pink* with a *purple band* around the openings where water comes and goes.

WAXY TROPICAL FLATWORM   2 in.

This tropical species is often seen feeding on clusters of tunicates. It is pale brown with *wavy dark brown lines.* Flatworms are simple animals that have only one body opening, where food goes in and waste comes out.

RED-BANDED FANWORM   6 in.

A segmented worm that is recognized by the *bright red,* fan-shaped appendages that give the worm its popular name, "feather duster worm." It lives in a tough fibrous tube that it constructs, revealing only its head to fan the water and capture prey.

FLAT TREE OYSTER   3 in.

These *flat gray* oysters often cover whole sections of mangrove roots. Like the tunicates, they are permanently attached and filter their food from the currents.

COLLARED SAND ANEMONE   3 in.

Looking like a tentacled mass of jelly, this greenish anemone is common among the mangrove roots, but it is often overlooked because it is partially buried in the sand. It has a flattened disk with *radiating furrows.*

MANGROVE
TUNICATE

PAINTED
TUNICATE

WAXY TROPICAL
FLATWORM

FLAT
TREE OYSTER

RED-BANDED
FANWORM

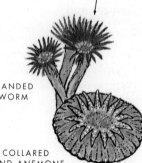

COLLARED
SAND ANEMONE

Many kinds of fish, especially young ones, lurk among the sheltering roots of the mangroves.

SERGEANT MAJOR   7 in.

Juvenile Sergeant Majors are among the most common fish on coral reefs and in mangrove swamps. Usually seen in schools, they have *black bands* lining their *yellowish sides,* somewhat like the stripes of an army sergeant major. These fish lay eggs in protected crevices, and males guard the eggs. The males turn much darker when guarding eggs.

SCHOOLMASTER   24 in.

The Schoolmaster is a member of the snapper family, known to be tasty fishes. It is *pale yellow* with *yellow fins* and has a *dark line* from the front of its face through its eye to its forehead. Schoolmasters are carnivorous, and snap up tiny plankton from among the mangrove roots. Juveniles are most common among the mangroves. When mature, Schoolmasters live in Turtle Grass meadows (see p. 102) and on the coral reef.

REDFIN NEEDLEFISH   24 in.

This slender fish is shaped much like a dart and lives just below the water surface. It often jumps from the water and may be mistaken for a flyingfish. It is quite stream-lined, with a *long mouth* and *red upper fins.* The upper and lower jaws are the same length. Needlefish are predators, feeding on tiny fish and plankton near the water surface.

BALLYHOO   16 in.

Ballyhoos are recognized by their very *long lower jaw* and short upper jaw. Like needle-fish, they stay just below the surface and are swift swimmers that quickly snap up tiny planktonic animals. Ballyhoos are less slender than needlefish, and the upper part of their tail is *orange.*

juvenile
SERGEANT MAJOR

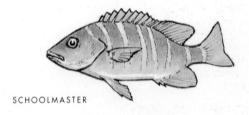

SCHOOLMASTER

BALLYHOO

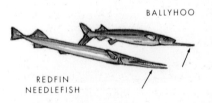

REDFIN
NEEDLEFISH

Turtle Grass Meadows

Turtle Grass is a marine grass that grows on warm coral sands protected by reefs. Many animals, including sea turtles such as the **Hawksbill,** live in these undersea meadows. Schools of fish, such as the **Stoplight Parrotfish** and **Rainbow Parrotfish,** graze like finny cattle on the coral sand. The sound of their sand-crunching can be heard by snorkelers. Some male Stoplight Parrotfish are brilliant turquoise with yellow spots.

Schools of blue-and-yellow-striped **French Grunt** share the Turtle Grass with the parrotfish. Grunt, like many other fish, can make a sound with their swim bladders, hence their name. Probing among the sand grains with a thin tentacle from its lower jaw, the **Spotted Goatfish** seeks tiny worms and other food.

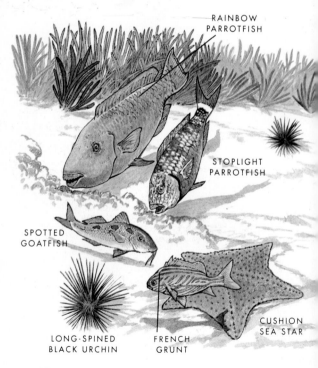

RAINBOW PARROTFISH

STOPLIGHT PARROTFISH

SPOTTED GOATFISH

LONG-SPINED BLACK URCHIN

FRENCH GRUNT

CUSHION SEA STAR

The delicate, brilliantly colored juvenile **Cocoa Damselfish** lives in abandoned shells of **Queen Conchs**. This little iridescent purple and yellow fish will retreat quickly to its shell when threatened.

When wading among Turtle Grass, keep an eye out for the **Long-spined Black Urchin.** The sharp spines are poisonous and painful, like the sting of a wasp. Another fearsome creature of the Turtle Grass is the **Great Barracuda,** a sleek silvery blue fish that can reach lengths of 3 feet but is usually smaller. These fish look dangerous but rarely attack humans.

In contrast to the bold and active barracudas, the **Donkey Dung Sea Cucumber** and **Cushion Sea Star** are utterly peaceful looking as they rest in the coral sand among the Turtle Grass.

TURTLE GRASS HAWKSBILL

GREAT BARRACUDA

DONKEY DUNG SEA CUCUMBER

QUEEN CONCH

COCOA DAMSELFISH

The Coral Reef

Corals are tiny animals related to sea anemones. They live in warm tropical waters and
form vast colonies called reefs. In our area,
coral reefs are found in southern Florida and
the Florida Keys, and throughout the Caribbean. Coral animals secrete calcium carbonate, a hard rocky material in which the
coral animals are embedded. Like tiny anemones, most corals capture plankton with
stinging cells in their ring of tentacles.

The reef serves as habitat for vast numbers
of colorful fish and invertebrates. Reef waters
are normally clear, and the best way to see the
rich life of the reef is to snorkel leisurely at the
surface, enjoying the undersea show below.

STAGHORN and ELKHORN CORALS
These corals are abundant in shallow
waters. They are shaped much like shrubs
with many branches. Staghorns are identified by their multitudes of *thin, sharp
branches.* Elkhorns have *wide, flattened
branches.*

BOULDER CORAL   5 ft.
This coral is often quite large, like its name-
sake. It is abundant throughout the Caribbean.

ROSE CORAL   3 in.
Named for its resemblance to the flower,
Rose Coral is yellowish, with *wavy edges.*
Look for it while snorkeling over beds of
Turtle Grass.

RED CORAL   1/2 in.
This small coral is easily recognized by its
red color. The coral animals, called polyps,
are, like many corals, active mostly at night.

BRAIN CORAL   5 ft.
Named for its obvious resemblance to a
human brain. Some brain corals are quite
large, like boulder corals, and all have *wavy
grooves.*

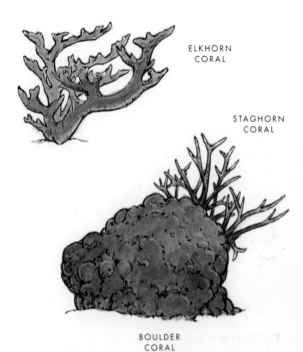

ELKHORN
CORAL

STAGHORN
CORAL

BOULDER
CORAL

ROSE
CORAL

RED CORAL

BRAIN
CORAL

FIRE CORAL

Not a true coral, Fire Coral is closely related to the dangerous Portuguese Man-Of-War. If you brush against it, the sensation is similar to stinging nettle. Fire Coral has flattened tan branches with *pale yellow edges.*

FIREWORM   To 12 in.

Like Fire Coral, the little Fireworm has a highly irritating sting. Common thoughout reefs, Fireworms are olive with *red bristles* with *white tips.* This colorful worm is to be observed but not handled.

TAN BUSHY SOFT CORAL

Though this animal is a true coral, it lacks a bonelike support. It waves gently in the currents, looking more like a shrub than an animal colony.

TRUMPETFISH   3 ft.

These *long, thin* fish have long jaws and a *blunt snout.* They are usually seen resting vertically among soft coral branches. Like many fish, they can change color but are usually tan or rich brown with *blue spots.*

SEA FANS

These well-named soft corals are *wide and flat.* Their main branches are connected by an *intricate latticework.* Color varies, but they are often purple.

FLAMINGO TONGUE   1 in.

This snail lives among sea fans and soft corals, feeding on the tiny coral animals. It is *spotted with orange and black* and has a *ridge* around the center of the shell.

GIANT TUBE SPONGE   3 ft.

A large sponge that looks like a cluster of long *bluish or reddish cylinders.*

STRAWBERRY SPONGE   8 in.

A *deep red* sponge, rounded, with *bumps* on its surface.

IRIDESCENT TUBE SPONGE   To 12 in.

Glowing orange, pink, purple, or blue, and very *wrinkled.*

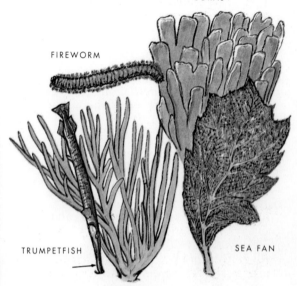

FIRE
CORAL

FIREWORM

TRUMPETFISH

TAN BUSHY
SOFT CORAL

SEA FAN

FLAMINGO
TONGUE

STRAWBERRY
SPONGE

IRIDESCENT
TUBE SPONGE

GIANT TUBE
SPONGE

Fish and Other Coral-reef Animals

QUEEN ANGELFISH   **10 in.**

Angelfish have a round shape, with long
tapering fins. The Queen is generally yellow
with an *all yellow tail*. Body edged with blue,
with a *black "crown"* atop the head.

ROCK BEAUTY   **8 in.**

This angelfish has a *deep yellow face* and
black sides. Like other angelfish, Rock
Beauties are generally slow moving and solitary, and use their blunt mouths to feed
mostly on sponges.

SPOTFIN BUTTERFLYFISH   **8 in.**

This common butterflyfish is white and
yellow with a *bold black spot* near its tail
and a prominent *black line through its eye*.
Butterflyfish are related to angelfish and are
equally brilliant in color. With their slender,
protruding jaws, they feed on tiny animals
and plants snipped from the surface of the
corals.

BLUE TANG   **9 in.**

Blue Tang are often found swimming in
large schools among the corals, where they
eat mostly algae. Like many coral reef
fishes, young Tang look quite different from
the adults of their species. Tang are *deep
blue* when they are fully grown but *bright
yellow* as juveniles. They are members of a
family called surgeonfishes, all of which
have a sharp spine at the base of the tail
that is used for defense. Surgeonfishes are
poisonous to humans.

QUEEN
ANGELFISH

ROCK
BEAUTY

SPOTFIN
BUTTERFLYFISH

juvenile

adults

BLUE TANG

PORKFISH   15 in.

Porkfish are among the most colorful of the colorful reef fishes. They have a sharply angled head with *two wide black stripes,* one of which goes through the eye, the other through the gills. Fins are yellow, and pale blue and yellow stripes run along the body. These fish often swim in large schools over the reef. Porkfish are members of a family called grunts, because they have teeth deep in their throats that they grind together to make a low, grunting sound. Porkfish are quite tasty.

QUEEN TRIGGERFISH   24 in.

The Queen Triggerfish has a spine on top of its head. The spine is flattened against the back, but can be suddenly and forcefully erected to startle would-be predators. Triggerfish usually swim alone, slowly sculling along using their *large* upper and lower fins. This *long-snouted* fish feeds on sea urchins, poking its narrow, strong mouth between the sharp spines. Color varies; some Queen Triggerfish are very dark, but most that live on coral reefs have *blue bodies with yellow faces,* usually striped with blue.

SPANISH HOGFISH   15 in.

Hogfish have sloping heads that can be poked into coral crevices. They belong to a large family called the wrasses, and are mostly solitary, feeding on a variety of small fish and other animals. Adult Spanish Hogfishes are *orangy red* above and toward the front and *brilliant yellow* below and to the back. Young fish are *blue* above but yellow on the sides, belly, and tail.

SQUIRRELFISH   12 in.

The Squirrelfish is *silvery red* with *huge black eyes.* On its back it has a spiny fin and a smooth, tapered fin. It has a deeply notched tail. There are many species of squirrelfish and most look alike. They spend the day tucked in among the coral heads, emerging to feed at night.

PORKFISH

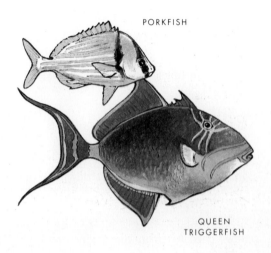

QUEEN
TRIGGERFISH

SPANISH
HOGFISH

SQUIRRELFISH

NASSAU GROUPER   To 3 ft.

This is a large member of the bass family. It is usually pale tan or gray with *wide dark stripes*. Many groupers are good to eat. They can change sex— small ones are females at first, but change into males as they grow.

PEPPERMINT SHRIMP   1 1/2 in.

These small *red and white striped* shrimp have long legs and long antennae, and prominent black eyes. They delicately crawl about on corals in search of tiny prey.

BLUEHEAD   7 in.

This member of the wrasse family is one of the most common small reef fishes. Only some males, called supermales, have the *blue head*. Other males and all females are smaller and are generally yellow with dark blotches. Wrasses sometimes change sex— females may turn into supermales.

Both the Peppermint Shrimp and Bluehead remove parasites from many kinds of fish. Called cleaners, these animals obtain food by removing irritating parasites from the mouths of fish such as the Nassau Grouper. In spite of the fact that the cleaners would make an easy meal for the grouper, it never eats them. Many other large reef fish permit cleaners free rein, even opening their mouths for the cleaners. Both animals benefit: the cleaners get fed, and the large fish is cleaned of parasites. When two or more animals interact in such a way that each benefits, the relationship is called symbiosis.

SPINY LOBSTER   24 in.

Though it lacks the big, meaty claws of its northern counterpart, the Spiny Lobster is a popular seafood. The shell, or carapace, is usually *reddish brown*. The antennae are covered with *sharp spines*. Spiny Lobsters sometimes gather and form long lines, one lobster clinging to the next, and migrate many miles. This strange migration may be a way for the lobsters to find suitable mates.

NASSAU
GROUPER

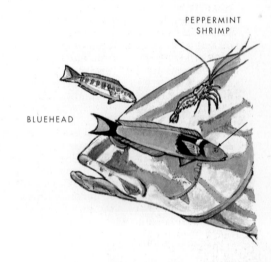

PEPPERMINT
SHRIMP

BLUEHEAD

SPINY
LOBSTER

ARROW CRABS   2 in.

Arrow Crabs are extremely slender crabs that are *striped* yellow and brown with *purple or blue* claws. Their name comes from their *sharply pointed* head, shaped somewhat like the tip of an arrow. Their legs are very long, giving them a delicate look when they walk. Look for them in coral crevices, where they feed on tiny animals and waste material.

SLIMY BRITTLE STAR   4 in.

This colorful *reddish orange* brittle star is one of several common brittle stars found on coral reefs. Brittle stars, unlike sea stars, are *very active* and will curl their delicate arms around your fingers. The name brittle star refers to the fact that their arms break off quite easily, but if this happens, a new arm will eventually grow. The Slimy Brittle Star feels slimy, but it is quite harmless. Brittle stars are predators, feeding on many kinds of small mollusks and worms.

ATLANTIC OVAL SQUID   10 in.

These common squid, also called Reef Squid, are frequently curious about snorkelers, and small schools will swim up to take a close look. The fins along the animals' sides *ripple* as they swim by. Color is mostly *purple* but may be *pale yellow with purple dots*. Tentacles are *short* and, like all squid, these animals can swim equally well backward or forward. They feed on shrimp and other animals.

INFLATED SEA BISCUIT   5 in.

A sea biscuit is an echinoderm, related to sea urchins, and is covered by *small spines.* In shape it does indeed resemble a biscuit, being rounded and somewhat *puffy.* Color varies, and it may be yellow, brownish, or red. Common on Turtle Grass beds, it is often well camouflaged and hard to see. Sea biscuits feed on waste material and tiny plants.

ARROW
CRAB

SLIMY
BRITTLE STAR

ATLANTIC
OVAL SQUID

INFLATED
SEA BISCUIT

Pacific Coast Seashores

From the Baja Peninsula north through California, Oregon, and Washington, West Coast seashores are home to a rich diversity of creatures. Among the mammals are the **California Sea Lion,** the **Elephant Seal,** and the **Sea Otter.** Unlike seals, sea lions have small external ears. They often sit upright, looking like dogs with flippers. Males weigh up to 660 pounds, and they bark quite loudly.

The large drooping snout of the adult male Elephant Seal is inflated in mating season. An adult male can weigh 3.5 tons. Elephant Seals are less common than sea lions, but both occur all along the Pacific Coast.

HEERMANN'S GULL

TUFTED PUFFIN

BLACK OYSTERCATCHER

The Sea Otter, once threatened with extinction, is now common along the northern Pacific Coast, where it feeds among the kelp beds. Sea Otters feed while floating on their backs, using a rock to crack open a mollusk or sea urchin.

Among the many kinds of birds on the western coast, look for the **Black Oystercatcher, Black Turnstone,** and **Wandering Tattler** probing about the intertidal zone. All are well camouflaged against black rocks and dark kelp. The slate gray **Heermann's Gull** is also common in rocky areas. Offshore islands are nesting sites for the colorful **Tufted Puffin,** with its orange-red bill and plume of yellow feathers.

ELEPHANT
SEAL

SEA OTTER

CALIFORNIA
SEA LION

WANDERING
TATTLER

BLACK
TURNSTONE

Pacific Coast Fishes

CALIFORNIA GRUNION   7 in.
The grunion is a slender fish that resembles
a sardine. It is greenish above with a *silvery
blue side stripe,* and silvery below. Grunion
spawn during high spring and summer
tides, when large numbers invade sandy
beaches to lay their eggs in the moist sand.

SOCKEYE SALMON   2–3 ft.
The Sockeye is also famous for its spawning
behavior. Sockeyes hatch in fresh water, but
they spend 1–4 years as adults in the sea.
When ready to spawn, they enter rivers and
swim upstream, often against swift currents, to breed where they hatched. Their
bodies are *bright red* with a *green head.*
Spawning fish develop strongly *curved jaws.*
After they spawn, these fish quickly perish.

WOLF-EEL   6 ft.
An often feisty fish that inhabits rocky areas
and is sometimes caught by rod and reel.
These long fish have sharp teeth, useful for
their diet of mollusks and fish, and they can
give a painful bite. They are grayish brown
with *dark spots outlined by pale rings.*

OPAH   4½ ft.
The odd-looking Opah, also called Moonfish
because of its round shape, is sometimes
hooked by salmon and tuna fishermen. It is
silvery blue with bright red fins and mouth.
Opahs feed on many kinds of fish as well as
squid and other invertebrates.

LEOPARD SHARK   5–7 ft.
This shark is a common inhabitant of
inshore sandy and rocky areas. A colorful
member of the shark tribe, it is identified by
its *black* bars, saddles, and spots.

PACIFIC ELECTRIC RAY   3–4½ ft.
A flat, *very round* fish, gray or brown, with
black spots. This common ray has special
muscle tissue that emits a strong electric
shock. It lives on sandy bottoms, often
buried in the sand, and in kelp beds.

CALIFORNIA
GRUNION

male

SOCKEYE
SALMON

WOLF-EEL

OPAH

LEOPARD
SHARK

PACIFIC
ELECTRIC RAY

Giant Kelp Forests

Several species of giant kelp thrive in the cool, nutrient-rich waters of the West Coast. These fast-growing brown algae may be anchored more than 300 feet below the surface, but even in the dark depths, their fronds capture more than enough of the sun's energy to sustain the entire plant. Dense "kelp forests" are habitat for many fish and invertebrates.

CALIFORNIA SHEEPHEAD 3 ft.
This fish is *black at both ends* and *red in the middle.* It feeds on a wide variety of hard-shelled invertebrates. Its population has unfortunately declined because of over-hunting by spear-fishers.

GARIBALDI 14 in.
This *brilliant orange* fish is unmistakable. It frequents rocky areas and caves as well as kelp forests where it feeds on invertebrates. Garibaldis are territorial, and make an audible thumping sound if disturbed. This fish is protected in California, making it illegal to catch it.

CHINA ROCKFISH 30 in.
Rockfish inhabit rocky areas and kelp beds. They have sharp spines on their upper fin that can inflict an irritating wound. The China Rockfish is bluish black, speckled with yellow, with a *wide yellow stripe* on its side. It is one of the tastiest of rockfishes.

ROUGHEYE ROCKFISH 3 ft.
A very large rockfish, the Rougheye is *bright red* with a *huge eye.* It stays in deeper water, where its red color reflects no light, rendering it virtually invisible.

KELP ROCKFISH 18 in.
This is a shallow-water species. Its *olive green* color is a good camouflage among the kelp fronds.

KELP
ROCKFISH

GIANT KELP

CALIFORNIA
SHEEPHEAD

GARIBALDI

CHINA
ROCKFISH

ROUGHEYE
ROCKFISH

Tide Pools

Beachcombing is rewarding all along the West Coast. Head for rocky areas to look for tide pools full of different kinds of algae, invertebrates, and fish.

PURPLE SEA STAR   8 in.
The Purple Sea Star has five arms and may vary in color from *purple to bright orange.*

SUN STAR   To 34 in.
The Sun Star may be almost *three feet wide* and has up to *24 arms,* making it one of the largest sea stars. It is usually pink but may be orange. Sea stars feed on mollusks.

GREEN SEA URCHIN   4 in.
This species, as well as the next, is often abundant in rocky tidal areas. Named for its uniform *olive green* color, the Green Sea Urchin is found most often in calm waters.

PURPLE SEA URCHIN   4 in.
Purple Sea Urchins are found in rougher waters. They are *dark red to violet* in color. Both the Purple and Green sea urchins eat large quantities of kelp and are in turn eaten in large numbers by Sea Otters.

GIANT SEA CUCUMBER   18 in.
This echinoderm of western rocky shores is identified by its *large size, yellow tentacles,* and *short yellow spines.*

GOOSE BARNACLES   2 in.
Clumps of these common barnacles are often attached to rocks and flotsom. They are recognized by their "necks," which are *muscular stalks* for attachment. The name comes from the 16th-century notion that geese hatched from the egg-shaped shells.

EDIBLE CRAB   9 in.
This *purplish brown* crab inhabits sandy areas, where it often burrows, leaving only its eyes and antennae exposed. Like most all crabs, it is both a predator and scavenger. People find it very tasty.

PURPLE
SEA STAR

SUN STAR

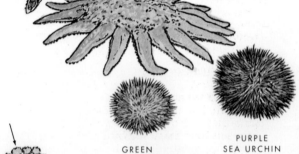

GREEN
SEA URCHIN

PURPLE
SEA URCHIN

GIANT
SEA CUCUMBER

GOOSE
BARNACLES

EDIBLE
CRAB

GREEN SEA ANEMONE   4 in.

This *bright green* anemone is often abundant in tide pools, where it eats small fish.

SEA PEN   12 in.

Sea Pens are related to sea anemones, and large colonies live in sandy waters below tide line. Sea pens have a *long stalk* and *many horizontal branches* with tiny tentacles for capturing planktonic animals.

LINED RED CHITON   1¹/₂ in.

Chitons are mollusks that are covered by 8 plates. They occur on both coasts, but more species are found along the West Coast. This common chiton is orange-red with *wavy black lines.*

GIANT PACIFIC CHITON   12 in.

Easily the largest of the chitons, its eight bony plates are normally covered by *orange-red flesh.* Chitons attach firmly to rocks to withstand wave pounding. They eat algae.

PINK ABALONE   8 in.

Abalones are an odd family of snails found along the Pacific Coast. They are known for their delicious flavor and are popular on restaurant menus. Their shells are flat, with 4–6 holes for venting water and waste material. They cling tightly to rocks, mostly feeding on kelp. The inside of their shells glistens with many iridescent colors. The Pink Abalone has a *wavy shell*, mostly *pinkish red.*

PACIFIC OCTOPUS   24–36 in.

A mollusk, the octopus is related to squid but lives among rocks and in caves rather than in the open sea. An octopus has 8 tentacles, each with two rows of suckers. It feeds on crabs, clams, and snails, cracking them open with its sharp beak that is much like a bird's. Pacific Octopus is usually *dark reddish* with arms 2–3 feet long, though some large individuals have arms up to 14 feet long.

GREEN
SEA ANEMONE

LINED
RED CHITON

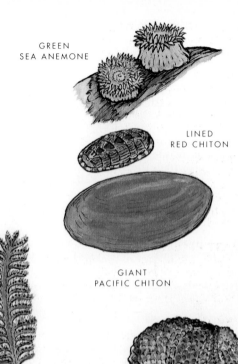

GIANT
PACIFIC CHITON

PINK
ABALONE

SEA PEN

PACIFIC
OCTOPUS

Off Pacific Shores

A day on a boat offshore from the West Coast can bring you close to some of the Earth's most magnificent animals. From November to May, watch for pods of **Gray Whales** (to 45 ft.) on their annual migration. The world's largest animal is the **Blue Whale,** which may be 100 feet long. A newborn calf may be 20 feet long. Both of these species have begun to recover from near-extinction caused by hunting. These immense animals feed on tiny shrimp-like krill, which they harvest by the billions. Packs of black and white **Killer Whales,** or Orcas (to 35 ft.), occasionally prey on Blue Whales, but more often feed on fish, seals, and sea lions. Often gliding gracefully near the water's surface, close to feeding whales, the **Black-footed Albatross** has a wingspan of up to 7 feet. Albatrosses feed on fish and squid.

BLACK-FOOTED
ALBATROSS

KILLER
WHALE

GRAY
WHALE

BLUE
WHALE

Index

128